Representations of Palestine in Egyptian Cinema

CINEMA AND MEDIA CULTURES IN THE MIDDLE EAST

Terri Ginsberg and Chris Lippard
Series Editors

Vol. 1

Claire Begbie

Representations of Palestine in Egyptian Cinema

Politics of (In)visibility

PETER LANG
Lausanne • Berlin • Bruxelles • Chennai • New York • Oxford

Library of Congress Cataloging-in-Publication Control Number: 2023002438

Bibliographic information published by the **Deutsche Nationalbibliothek.**
The German National Library lists this publication in the German
National Bibliography; detailed bibliographic data is available
on the Internet at http://dnb.d-nb.de.

Cover design by Peter Lang Group AG

ISSN 2770-9051 (print)
ISSN 2770-9043 (online)
ISBN 9781433188404 (hardback)
ISBN 9781433188527 (ebook)
ISBN 9781433188534 (epub)
DOI 10.3726/b18395

Published by Peter Lang Publishing Inc., New York, USA
info@peterlang.com - www.peterlang.com

This publication has been peer reviewed.

Epigraph

What we must again see is the issue involving *representation*, an issue always lurking near the question of Palestine.

(Edward Said, *The Question of Palestine*, 39)

And so a rift began to form in Egypt on the issue of Palestine, not on the matter of sympathy for the Palestinians but as to what Egypt's political involvement should be.

(Leila Ahmed, *A Border Passage*, 259)

Table of Contents

List of Figures

Preface

I would like to preface this book with a brief word about the academic training and positionality that circumscribe its approach and focus. While it makes evident steps into Film Studies, an academic discipline that has gradually increased its attention to Arab cinema during the past couple of decades, the book started out as a Middle East Studies project—albeit out of a willingness to critique some of the very limitations inherent to area studies, with its colonial and Cold War origins, and some of its more recent, neoliberal directions. To critically center Palestine across different academic disciplines is a perceived and very real need—as a necessary means to resist and counter the insidious effects of the normalization of Zionism and neoliberalism. Doing so inevitably entails pushing certain boundaries and critiquing transnational systems of power into which we are unevenly slotted and in which we therefore have differential capacities, responsibilities, and ways of acting. As a transnationally positioned researcher from the Global North, my work has been conditioned by certain privileges, will comprise constraints but may also prompt new insights, questions and critiques. As a visitor to the book subject's geographical site and culture, I take responsibility for any errors, inaccuracies or missed cultural references and make no pretense to definitive conclusions. At the same time, I hope to convey my enduring affinity for the Arabic language and its wealth of cultural production as well as my commitment to teasing out some of the contradictions and processes of negotiation underpinning international relations and their cinematic mediation.

Acknowledgments

The first seeds of this project were unknowingly sown 8 years ago when I was lucky enough to study in Palestine for a year and immerse myself in Palestinian literature and cinema. The book's current shape, however, is the product of an ongoing learning trajectory, informed by many classes and readings, generous scholars and academics, and conversations with peers and neighbors who have all left traces in my thinking and writing.

Many people have been directly or indirectly involved in the gestation and development of this project. To begin with, I would like to thank the two series editors, Dr. Terri Ginsberg and Dr. Chris Lippard, for encouraging and supporting this publication, as well as Peter Lang Publishing for their institutional support.

This project would not have come into being, let alone developed, without the consistent encouragement and mentorship of Dr. Terri Ginsberg, whose course on Palestinian cinema at The American University in Cairo (AUC) first inspired this project, and whose film theoretical scholarship and ongoing conversations with me about cinema and politics have brought ideas, form and structure to my research.

I would also like to thank Dr. Surti Singh, who generously supervised an Andrew Mellon Grant post-MA fellowship at AUC that allowed me to begin working on this publication.

At my current institution, Concordia University, Dr. Masha Salazkina has offered valuable time and constructive feedback, which significantly helped me improve earlier drafts of this manuscript. Dr. Kay Dickinson's insightful class on Arab revolution cinema and feedback on my research and writing have contributed further sources of inspiration and support, for which I am very grateful.

I would also like to thank Viviane Saglier, Chloe Bordewich, Giuseppe Fidotta, Sima Kokotović and Ilona Jurkonytė for closely reading draft chapters and providing generative feedback that have undoubtedly improved the final product and have pushed me to deepen my research and writing skills.

To the many professors and teachers from whom I have had the privilege to learn during the past few years, many thanks for your valuable insights, scholarship, and intellectual generosity. At AUC, I was fortunate to be in the classes of several exceptional professors, whose scholarship—even though at the time I had no idea I would go on to write a book—laid the foundations for my ongoing interests and interdisciplinary inclinations, and who always pointed me in the right direction while I was still finding my feet intellectually. While this work may not directly line up with their own scholarly interests and expertise, or necessarily reflect their views, I owe my sincere gratitude to Drs. Iman Hamam, Pascale Ghazaleh, Ferial Ghazoul, Samia Mehrez, and Samah Selim who, each in her own way, contributed immensely to my intellectual growth. I would also like to thank film critic and scholar, Nour El Safoury, whose highly engaging course on Egyptian popular cinema at the Cairo Institute of Liberal Arts and Sciences (CILAS) added many more ideas and layers to my knowledge as I continued to learn much more about this rich cinematic tradition.

Without the patience and kindness of Radwa Wassim working at AUC's Middle East Studies Center, I would likely not have persevered throughout challenging writing times. I would also like to thank my fellow peers and friends, many of whom were either around in the earliest stages of this project or offered emotional support and laughter in the later writing stages: Norhan, Nourhan, Diana, Sara, Nesma, Mai, Nada, and Hoza, as well as my flatmates and friends Ayah, Banan, Rasha, Heba, Amany, Jomana, Khaled, Inji, Ingy, Mo, Isabella, Yulia, Paolo, Alexandra, Naima—and not to forget my dearest neighbors, Iman, Halima and Jakob.

Living a bit of a nomadic existence has meant that a lot of friends live further afield or have only recently come into my life, but every one of them has in different capacities supported me along the way. Thanks to Lamisse, Imane, Fatima, Raffi, Ricarda, Laura, Saffa, Aurelia, Rahel, my PhD cohort at Concordia, Fadi and Lilia for welcoming me to Montreal, as well as Afshan for her generosity and the writing group for offering consistent motivation.

Finally, thanks to my family for always being there, showing unconditional support and fostering my early interest in language, literature and cinema.

List of Abbreviations

ARTE	Association Relative à la Télévision Européenne
CFF	Carthage Film Festival
CSI	Cinema Support Institution
EMG	Egyptian Media Group
ICP	Iraqi Communist Party
IDF	Israeli Defense Forces
IMF	International Monetary Fund
NFO	National Film Organization
PA	Palestinian Authority
PDFLP	Popular Democratic Front for the Liberation of Palestine
PFLP	Popular Front for the Liberation of Palestine
PFU	Palestine Film Unit
PLO	Palestine Liberation Organization
QIZ	Qualifying Industrial Zone
RCC	Revolutionary Command Council
UAR	United Arab Republic
UNRWA	United Nations Relief and Works Agency
VGIK	The Gerasimov Institute of Cinematography (Moscow)

Introduction

The Palestinian struggle for liberation, justice and national self-determination has, throughout much of the twentieth and twenty-first centuries, formed the cornerstone of Middle Eastern geopolitics, with Egypt crucially implicated at several key moments since the 1948 *Nakba* (catastrophe), when the settler-colonial state of Israel was established in historic Palestine, replacing the British Mandate (1918–48). Located at the historical crossroads of the three major Abrahamic religions (Judaism, Christianity, Islam) and in close geographical proximity to significant oil reserves in the region, Palestine/Israel has come to form a central political issue for its southwestern neighbor, Egypt, as well as a site of discord and opposition which successive Egyptian governments have instrumentalized in their quests to construct, enact and legitimate a particular (pan/trans)nationalist ideology, garner popular support and manage the country's position within the regional and global political economy. These conditions have led Egypt to align itself strategically with different global powers, in particular juggling the United States and the Soviet Union during the Cold War or, in the increasingly globalized, neoliberal post-Cold War era, forming a mutually profitable alliance with the U.S.–Israel–Saudi Arabia bloc. Since the Nakba, Egypt has endured several direct confrontations with the Israeli aggressor (1948, 1956, 1967, 1973) as well as played a significant mediating role for Palestine, whether that be as a host state for exiled Palestinians, as an early patron of the nascent Palestinian liberation movement from the 1960s onward, or when—in the context of negotiating the "peace process" inaugurated between Egypt and Israel at Camp David in 1978 and culminating in the ultimate failure, of the eventual 1995 Oslo II Accords brokered in Taba, Egypt—recognizing a form of limited Palestinian self-rule under the nascent Palestinian Authority (PA).[1]

In justified response to the gradual normalization of the Israeli occupation[2] that has deprived generations of Palestinians of their basic rights to freedom of movement, self-determination and sovereignty over their land and properties, and the settlement expansion of which has perpetually violated international law, the ceaseless instances of political resistance practiced by the Palestinian people are a testament to the lengthy history and unresolved status of the Palestinian struggle. This struggle has inspired the formation and growth of a regional base of Arab popular support that dates to the earliest stages of Zionist colonization of Palestine at the beginning of the twentieth century and would have international reverberations by the late 1960s during a period of heightened global anti-imperialist sentiment and solidarity with oppressed peoples around the world.

Yet Egypt's hegemonic position in the Arab region has clearly been intricately tied to, and in turn threatened by, its historically inconsistent and, since the late 1970s, increasingly conciliatory diplomatic relationship with Israel and the latter's transnational supporters. Vocal supporters of the Palestinian struggle, skeptics and opponents of Egyptian foreign policy with respect to Israel have tended to integrate criticism of Israel into broader anti-imperialist and anti-capitalist frameworks, with the intelligentsia in particular noting likely interconnections between the Egyptian military apparatus' accumulation of capital, its profitable alliance with the United States, and the state's compromises with Israel during this period. The tensions and contradictions which this relationship has unleashed can also be mapped within the broad sphere of media and culture, perhaps most prominently in Egyptian cinema, an industry that has historically constituted a vital component of Egypt's cultural economy and has facilitated and helped consolidate Egypt's regional hegemony and popularity, leading to and, in turn, fueled by the wide cinematic export of the popular Egyptian vernacular across the Arabic-speaking world. Indeed, popular perceptions and support for the Palestinian cause have been comparatively consistent, even as Egypt's official policies vis-à-vis Palestine have fluctuated and adopted different forms over the years. The phenomenon of Egyptian cinematic representation of Palestine thus compels us to scrutinize state–society relations and make the important distinction between government and people—especially when talking about popular sentiment and social struggle. The fact that historic Palestine constitutes a crucial holy site for the Muslim world at large (being home to the Al-Aqsa Mosque in Jerusalem), and is a nodal point within the Arab nationalist imaginary, renders cinema—with its capacity to cross borders and foster imagined communities[3]—a particularly apt mass culture institution by which to examine more closely Egypt's imbrication within the Palestinian issue. *Representations of Palestine in Egyptian Cinema: Politics of (In) visibility* offers a segue into this relationship by considering how, at which key moments, and to what critical extent Egyptian cinema has historically engaged with the subject of Palestine.

Established during the colonial-monarchical period in the early twentieth century, when the Egyptian independence struggle was beginning to consolidate, and comprising a prolific corpus of films (primarily melodramas, comedies and musicals), Egyptian cinema has been at the forefront of developing, articulating and cultivating an Egyptian national imaginary. This has entailed the construction of numerous gendered, classed, racialized, and religious "others" into interpellative functions. As a technologically determined ideological apparatus embedded in capitalist circuits of exchange, Egyptian cinema has also inscribed and channeled many of the twentieth century's global aesthetic and discursive trends more generally. Yet despite boasting the region's oldest and most prolific cultural industry, and notwithstanding the fact that the loss of Palestine has been of vital and shared concern for Egyptians across the social and political spectrum, the direct and explicit treatment of the Palestinian issue has been relatively marginal within Egyptian cinema. As Terri Ginsberg (2016) has argued,

> It is indeed fair to say that Palestine not only comprises a predominant concern of modern Arab cinema but forms an allegorical core of the popular commercial cinema of the Middle East region. Due to state censorship resulting from government collaboration and/or compromise with Israel and U.S. pressure, however, central and sustained focus on the issue within the mainstream of Middle Eastern cinematic production has appeared less often than might be expected.[4]

Building upon this preliminary observation by looking at a range of films produced under changing politico-historical conditions across half a century, this book aims to trace and analyze how Egyptian cinema has imagined, engaged with, and represented Palestine across three paradigmatic moments within the evolving Egypt–Palestine/Israel nexus since 1948. In so doing, the book contributes to the scholarly discourse on Egypt's complex and shifting role in the broader Arab–Israeli conflict, as it lends particular attention to interconnections which may be ascertained between Egyptian foreign policy regarding Palestine, and popular struggles waged within the country's domestic sphere.[5] I shall analyze a selection of relevant films produced at three distinct historical moments representing significantly varying conditions of production—private sector–funded, state-funded, and transnationally co-funded. The aim of the book is to investigate how and to what extent Egypt's hegemonic status in the regional cinematic sphere has intersected the country's political commitment to Palestine—both on the official level of state policy, which has increasingly shifted toward normalization with Israel, and on the level of popular support, where solidarity with the Palestinian struggle has not significantly waivered and has in fact served to bridge marginalized concerns. Through a combination of textual analysis and politico-historical contextualization, the book theorizes this difficult and at times contradictory relationality and its ideology-effects in cinema. These ensuing *symptomatic readings* shall, more specifically, entail careful analysis of the films' generic conventions, their narrative-compositional structures and their thematic and symbolic significance with respect to Palestine.

Together, these readings will reveal that the representation of Palestine in Egyptian cinema has been intertwined symbiotically with Egypt's important role in the unfolding Palestinian struggle, whereupon the shifting conventions traceable within the subject films appear as critical effects of, or reactions to, the ideological status quo.[6] I argue that the changing signification of Palestine in Egyptian cinema has been overdetermined by Egypt's internal political struggles and their economic and geopolitical conditioning at respective historical moments, just as it has been informed by the technological and aesthetic transformations of the cinematic medium itself. Each chapter examines certain of these transformations, asking, for example, how important changes in Egyptian political economy are negotiated aesthetically and come to figure allegorically at the rhetorical and structural registers of the subject films, whether through melodramatic or realist conventions or via comparatively experimental expressions of diasporic fragmentation and dislocation.

Historical Scope and Context: Egyptian Political Economy and Hegemony

This short monograph thus traces an intersecting history of Egyptian cinema and politics with the Palestinian struggle. While the ensuing periodization spans 1948 to the present day, three paradigmatic moments are foregrounded: the years surrounding the 1952 Revolution, which saw Egypt's transition from monarchy to republic; the period of the post-1967 *Naksa* (setback), which signaled the retreat of President Gamal Abdel Nasser's pan-Arabist project; and the turn of the twenty-first century, by which time Egypt had not only normalized its diplomatic relationship with Israel but, under President Hosni Mubarak, had become fully integrated economically into the neoliberal capitalist order. Each of these moments marks a critical evolution within Egyptian–Palestinian relations as they involve the postcolonial history of the Arab region and major geopolitical shifts within the realm of global capitalism generally.

The Nakba signifies a critical turning point in modern Middle Eastern history. It names the violent culmination, in the form of ethnic cleansing, of the gradual Zionist encroachment and expropriation of Palestinian land and properties, the Israeli takeover of which irreversibly transformed the region's landscape and social fabric and produced large exilic Palestinian populations in neighboring Arab countries and beyond. The Nakba was but the first of many eruptions of Israeli settler-colonial violence in Palestine; indeed, the Nakba has been an ongoing catastrophe, setting into motion a tireless cycle of official (dis)agreements and (re) negotiations that have since resulted in the constant deferral of a just solution to the indefinite future, thus fostering a communal enmity and perpetually denying exiled and diasporic Palestinians their internationally mandated right to return home. A second critical turn in the Palestinian struggle occurred during the 1967 Naksa, which resulted in the Israeli occupation of the Jordanian-controlled West Bank, the Egyptian military-administered Gaza Strip, the Syrian (Golan/al-Jawlan) Heights, and the Sinai Peninsula in Egypt, and brought about another large expulsion of Palestinians into neighboring Arab countries. Most of these violent actions have implicated bordering Arab states and other external powers, not least of them Egypt, whose signing of the U.S.-brokered Camp David Accords under Anwar El Sadat in 1978—initiating normalization and an ongoing "peace process" with Israel—would have detrimental repercussions on the prospects for Palestinian liberation, marking a drastic shift away from a previously more supportive position under pan-Arab socialist president, Gamal Abdel Nasser, the relevant contradictions of whose regime—historical as well as structural—are nonetheless also inscribed across the Egyptian cinema of that period, as the ensuing chapters shall discuss.

In his *Representing Israel in Modern Egypt* (2012), Ewan Stein notes that Egyptian conceptions and representations of Israel in public discourse have been "closely related to the shifting political landscape in Egypt."[7] I will therefore first outline some key factors underpinning Egyptian political economy throughout the period under discussion, turning to a selection of Marxist texts that, focusing on Egypt, theorize changes and continuities in the role of its state apparatus in relation to its citizens by tracing the historical origins, patterns and events leading up to the 2011 popular uprising that toppled the autocratic presidency of Hosni Mubarak.[8] Many of these studies argue for a critical scrutiny of Egyptian class relations and their strategic importance for global capitalism and insist upon the fact that the postcolonial state continues to be shaped by the forces of imperialism.[9] Egypt's regional hegemony and influential role in the Arab–Israeli conflict are heavily contingent upon these structural conditions. Sean McMahon's (2017) dialectical history of Egyptian political economy in the throes of neoliberalism synthesizes these inextricable connections by focusing our attention on "the working class in relation to labor and capital on the global scale, and the particularities of Egyptian society in relation to the global neoliberal totality in crisis."[10] Other sources have looked at the endurance of a military regime since the transition from a colonially backed monarchy to a republic in 1952,[11] the anti-colonial moment around which the first chapter of this book pivots.

It is these political and economic conditions that shape, on a basic level, the shifting prism through which Palestine has come to figure in Egyptian cinema, from the anti-colonial moment of the early 1950s through the retreat of Nasserism in the late 1960s to the emergence and spread of transnational neoliberalism during latter decades of the twentieth century (an economic project that continues to govern the Egyptian mediascape into the present). This lengthy period, spanning over half a century, witnessed a concomitant shift from Egyptian (and other Arab) state patronage of the Palestinian cause, including support for Palestinian refugees, during the 1950s and early 1960s,[12] through the emergence during the late 1960s of a Palestinian armed struggle as a perceived antidote to the limited success of such patronage, to the popular rejection of the infamous Oslo Accords during the late 1990s, marked by the continuing First Palestinian Intifada which began in 1987. Today, three decades later, and seventy-five years since the Nakba, justice for Palestine is still pending.

Representing Palestine in Egypt and Beyond

While no scholarly paucity exists either on Egyptian popular media and culture, or the Palestinian issue in general, sustained research into their intersection across Egyptian cinema represents a critical lacuna. Several Arabic language works exist on the overarching subject, but their theorizations of the abiding intersection are lacking in deeper, critical analysis of film aesthetics.[13] Attention within the Anglophone literature—especially with respect to the early set of Egyptian films examined here—has also tended toward the cursory.[14]

From its very onset, the Palestinian issue has been subject to varying degrees of critical attention and mediation and has transcended multiple media, ranging from the press, literature, and music to the visual arts and, of course, cinema. Cinematic representations of Palestine in fact go back to the earliest stages of Zionist settlement of Arab lands in the early twentieth century, "begin(ning) virtually with cinema itself."[15] The current study focuses on a particular national cinematic representation of Palestine—that of Egypt, "the center of the theater of Arab public opinion"[16]—and in so doing references two main cognate bodies of academic literature that are useful as an intellectual basis for its inquiry: scholarship on the significance of Palestine within differing Arab and Egyptian media forms, and scholarship on Egyptian film and media representations of issues either indirectly related, or unrelated, to Palestine.

With respect to the first body of literature, Ghada Talhami's *Palestine in the Egyptian Press: From Al-Ahram to Al-Ahali* (2007) illustrates how Egyptian newspapers and journals have provided an insightful lens through which to observe the historical interaction of politics and representational culture.[17] It is Egyptian newspapers and magazines, according to Talhami, in which official and popular perceptions of Palestine and the ongoing sociopolitical effects of the Nakba are saliently revealed and constituted. For our purposes, these important media institutions arguably operate within similar politico-historical constraints as the Egyptian cinema industry. Not only has the Egyptian press, itself a national archive of historical events,[18] provided crucial "witness to history," but so too has cinema, in that it likewise comprises a reservoir of cultural references, official attitudes and popular perceptions, and thus testifies to the diverse and shifting ways in which Palestine has figured in the Egyptian national and political imaginary. Talhami's approach resembles that of postcolonial scholar Ella Shohat's *Israeli Cinema: East/West and the Politics of Representation* (1989), for which films are to be read "not as documents of fact but as registers of perceptions and perspectives on 'reality' and, simultaneously, as a means to actively shape that reality."[19]

The dynamic and politically attuned media of Egyptian and Arabic literature, poetry and music, and their engagement with the subject of Palestine, also provides generative context for this analysis.[20] Werner Ende's (1979) early survey of Palestine in contemporary Arabic literature demonstrates the shifting role of censorship in this area.[21] Likewise the censorship of Egyptian cinema has undergone transformation, including alternations, across successive political regimes, between relatively lenient measures of control and tighter regulations. In both instances, the advent of market-based imperatives toward audience reception—a phenomenon of capitalism—has posed formidable limits to expression in recent years. Regarding the musical field, the interplay of aesthetic form and manifest content in Palestinian songs has been discussed by Joseph Massad (2003), who observes that "the history of songs dealing with the Palestinian struggle parallels in many ways the history of the Palestinian struggle itself,"[22] once again offering an instructive parallel to this book's methodological approach to analyzing Egyptian cinema. Indeed, as we move from one politico-historical period to the next, we will find not only that the cinematic and narrative styles of the subject films alter—in line with developing technologies and global aesthetic trends—but that their dramatic themes evolve in ways that reflect the passage of time and thus refract the evolving historicity of the Palestinian struggle. In addition to serving as testament to the ongoing importance of Palestine within the popular Arab imaginary, that is, this array of cultural histories offers an overlapping series of templates for thinking about the Egypt–Palestine nexus *as* cultural production—of their parallel and intersecting national histories, so to speak. Here the meaningfulness of allegory as a representational device in Egyptian cinema bears mentioning. As Kay Dickinson (2007) fittingly puts it: "Allegory provides a way of picturing the unimaginably vast, be it the anonymous forces of global power struggles or the fantasized ideals of the national-populace-as-one. It connects and locks together entities whose alliance has perhaps been previously unimaginable."[23]

The other, main cognate body of academic literature that is useful for thinking methodologically about the Egyptian cinematic representation of Palestine comprises works that scrutinize the representation of other popular topics in Egyptian cinema, such as key political events and figures, the military, and the Arab nationalist project, to name but a few. These studies, while only tangentially or indirectly concerning Egyptian cinematic engagement with Palestine, are nonetheless relevant for what they reveal about Egyptian cinema history, its common periodization and generic conventions. For instance, Dalia Mostafa's *The Egyptian Military in Popular Culture* (2017) cannot circumvent Egyptian military involvement in successive Arab–Israeli wars and thus contains helpful references for a study centered more specifically on Egypt's changing role vis-à-vis Palestine. In analyzing the centrality of popular culture to nation-building and subject formation, and military figures as influential "heroes" in those processes, Mostafa complicates typically more simplified senses of how culture and the nation interact, albeit through a cultural thematic rather than film theoretical framework.[24] Viola Shafik's frequently cited work on Egyptian cinema, *Popular Egyptian Cinema* (2007),[25] and Lina Khatib's comparative study of American and Egyptian cinematic representations of Middle Eastern politics, *Filming the Modern Middle East* (2006),[26] are also noteworthy in this context, with the former framed around Egyptian cinema's representation of cultural difference (nation, gender, religion), and the latter interested in the constitution of hegemonic political subjectivity in relation to a range of issues including the "Arab–Israeli conflict" which, Khatib argues, is distinctly "spatialized" in Egyptian and American cinema, respectively.[27] These studies all relate the construction and evolution of Egyptian cinematic subjectivity to (un)conscious processes of othering—a central claim which the present study makes with respect to Egyptian cinematic representation of Palestine.

This book departs from these prior investigations, however, in that it seeks to articulate the Egyptian cinematic representation of Palestine more explicitly to the mentioned changes and continuities in political and economic conditions, and to critically analyze narrative-compositional structures, generic modes and aesthetic form as they encourage allegorical readings concerning the Egyptian relationship to Palestine. This book also departs from prior works in that it refrains from looking at Egyptian cinema from within a strictly national framework, although issues of national-popular identity and gendering processes of self-formation do, inevitably, come into play. Olivia Harrison's *Transcolonial Maghreb: Imagining Palestine in the Era of Decolonization* (2015), which draws upon Edward Said's *The Question of Palestine* (1992) in order to discuss "the global significance of Palestine,"[28] is relevant here for its argument that "Palestine is paradoxically illustrative of the (post)colonial condition."[29] More specifically, Harrison analyzes how the figure of Palestine as a "purportedly pan-Arab and pan-Islamic icon" has been deployed—in this case in Algeria—to formulate a critique of the state.[30] The present book, too, locates Palestine as an ideological site onto which shifting notions of Egyptian nationhood and politics are projected. It produces an epistemology of films that maps out shifts in Egyptian political economy, moving from a national and regional to a visibly global scale. Woven into this trajectory is a hermeneutic thread that analogizes the exilic movement of Palestinians, along with cinematic depictions of their struggle, to the development and shifting flows of transnational capital.

The growing body of literature on Palestinian cinema must not be left out of this contextualization. Palestinian cinema is both an increasingly established, if loosely construed, field of study and epitomizes a prolific transnational cinema. Acknowledging some of the recent publications in the area,[31] this book is in conversation with others of those which more closely explore the idea and practice of transnational solidarity in some capacity, whether explicitly regarding the visualization of Palestine solidarity,[32] the Palestine Revolution cinema of the long 1970s, to which many international filmmakers contributed,[33] or perspectives of travel and mobility.[34] Drawing upon these transnational approaches as they may hint at Egyptian cinema's relationship to Palestine, this book seeks to elaborate a more in-depth understanding of Egypt's imbrication in the Palestinian struggle and to outline a lengthier history of the subject in film. In building upon this extant body of literature, the crucial question emerges of whether the Egyptian films about Palestine discussed in this book may be considered works of solidarity, or whether it is instead necessary to see them, critically, as also engaged in the hegemonic practice of "othering."

As with any complex, politically and ideologically debated subject, that of this book could have taken different shapes and sizes. While I might have aimed for breadth by surveying and chronicling relevant films across an extensive time period, this book is less of a fact-gathering mission or a conclusive study; as such, evident strands of inquiry were intentionally left aside. For example, films produced in the 1960s by the Egyptian public sector, such as Youssef Chahine's crusader allegory of pan-Arab heroism, *Al-Nasser Salah Ad-Din* [*Saladin the Victorious*] (1963), and biopics that tackle key political events in the lives of Egyptian presidents, such as Mohamed Fadel's *Nasser 56* (1996) and Mohamed Khan's *Ayam al-Sadat* [*Days of Sadat*] (2001), or, in turn, films about prominent Palestinian figures such as Atef El Tayeb's *Nagi Al-Ali* (1991), about the Palestinian cartoonist, come to mind as films worthy of analysis in their own right and in terms of their politico-historical significance, and which have typically signaled high on the popular radar. I analyze here, instead, three paradigmatic cinematic moments for their capacity to elucidate a changing relationship between two neighboring national configurations entangled in a complex geopolitical struggle. As such this book engages *a*typical films from Egypt, yet those which are in fact among the most consistently referenced in relation to Palestine.[35]

Chapter Summaries

Seven feature-length films are the subject of this book's three chapters, while passing reference is made to others of relevance where appropriate. By way of an interdisciplinary approach, the selected films—which manifest differing generic conventions and aesthetic modalities—shall be analyzed with respect to their political-economic enabling conditions and the conventional development of the cinematic medium.

Chapter One locates the emergence of Palestine within a cluster of five Egyptian commercial melodramas that were produced from the late 1940s to mid-1950s. This emergence closely post-dated the Nakba in Palestine and spanned a similarly formative moment in Egyptian history: the period of the Free Officer's coup that ended the British-backed monarchy under King Farouk. At this point, Egypt's relationship to the newly established state of Israel was still being formulated, and the Egyptian private sector–run cinema industry was experiencing its first Golden Age, while still influenced by its colonial history in terms of institutional structure and generic and narrative conventions and amidst a gradual drive toward Egyptianization that had been underway since as early as the 1930s.

This chapter argues that Palestine became a symbolic issue for Egyptian nationalism at this historical moment, a fact made evident in a corresponding set of films that may be considered, as defined by Joel Gordon, "revolutionary melodramas."[36] Characteristic of these films is a sentimental, romantic love story intersecting with political events that led to and/or followed the Free Officers' revolution—in these instances in reference to the Palestine war of 1947–48. Palestine appears feminized in these films in the form of an Egyptian male protagonist's female love interest and serves as the central site of narrative conflict ("the war field"), where the heroic soldier—a Free Officer stand-in—struggles for liberation prior to his return to Egypt by film's end.

Through close reading and comparison of the films, the chapter will elucidate these allegorical figurations with respect to their ideological function—within the Egyptian melodramatic tradition more generally, and regarding Palestine in particular, while bearing in mind the genre's propensity to appeal to particular spectator positionalities as well as to produce commercial value. By critically attending to the labor that produces melodramatic excess—yet that also contains social contradictions—the chapter indicates, by extension, that while nationalist rhetoric and support for Palestine was able to unify Egyptians from across the political and ideological spectrum, the emerging national military state also contained challenges to its rule. Depicting Palestine from within the industrial form of melodrama, these lighthearted films obscure the broader political context of the Nakba, an effect which serves to dissimulate as entertainment the serious and more complex nature of the 1948 events.

Chapter Two examines Egypt's foreign policy trajectory with respect to the unfolding Palestinian struggle, by embedding an analysis of the critically acclaimed film, *Al-Makhdu'un* [*The Dupes*] (1972), directed by Egyptian filmmaker Tawfik Saleh and based on Palestinian writer Ghassan Kanafani's novella, *Rijal fi al-Shams* [*Men in the Sun*], in its politico-historical context: a high point of Cold War rivalries and a significant moment in the history of pan-Arabism, following the 1967 Six-Day War, known in Arabic as the Naksa and in common parlance as *al-Hazima* ("The Defeat"), in which victorious Israel took the West Bank from Jordan, the Golan Heights / al-Jawlan from Syria, and the Sinai Peninsula from Egypt. This last represented the crucial territorial asset to be traded for a peace treaty between Egypt and Israel several years later. The post-Naksa era signaled the breakdown of Nasser's pan-Arabism, including the dissolution of the United Arab Republic (UAR), a unity government between Egypt and Ba'thist Syria that had materialized in the context of Egypt's contemporary regional aspirations and amidst Nasser's attendant fear of communist ascendancy—a concern he shared with the Iraqi Ba'th. Despite Nasser's presenting the liberation of neighboring

Palestine as one of pan-Arabism's main objectives, the potentially independent Palestinian liberation movement that began to crystallize and organize across the Arab world—and that in fact had roots in Palestine during the 1930s, when the first pan-Arab party, Hizb al-Istiqlal (Independence Party), formed there in 1932—was quickly subsumed under his Egypt-led conception of unity between the Arab countries.

While the events of 1967 presented political setbacks for Egypt, they also paved the way for new political perspectives. Similarly, in the Egyptian cultural sector, the late 1960s was a period of collaborative spirit within artistic and intellectual circles, leading, for instance, to the emergence of a more oppositional and socially committed group of Arab filmmakers who formed part of a global left-wing cultural movement. Although a social realist tendency and interest in class relations had already emerged in Egyptian cinema from the 1930s, in films like *Al-Azima* [*Determination*] (1939), directed by Kamal Selim, filmmakers such as Tawfik Saleh innovated the genre by introducing a variation of neorealist aesthetic which, in its concern for the depiction of ordinary life and social struggles, critically contrasted Egypt's predominant melodramatic tradition. With respect to the representation of Palestine, this meant promoting a more grounded, critical perspective with which Palestinians would be able to identify.

Whereas *The Dupes* exemplifies this objective, its creation by an Egyptian filmmaker was not fostered under the aegis of the Egyptian industry. During the late Nasser years, Egyptian filmmakers like Saleh began to suffer from increasingly inefficient state bureaucracy and censorship, which compelled some of them to look for alternative ways and places to produce their films. Saleh, one of many artists to express discontent with Nasserism, migrated to the more tolerant Syria, where the public-sector National Film Organization (NFO) had actively summoned Arab filmmakers, offering sponsorship for more realistic and politicized narrations of the Palestinian struggle. Chapter Two considers the fact that *The Dupes* was the first pan-Arab production to center the Palestinian perspective while simultaneously projecting a self-reflexive critique of pan-Arabism. The film illustrates how, in the wake of the 1967 defeat, the unresolved Palestinian struggle became a popular locus for self-critique and inspired the creation of a more radical political aesthetic—one that challenged the generic conventions and escapist tendencies of commercial Egyptian melodrama and its complicity in the official rhetoric and political posturing of the Egyptian government. The film deploys symbolism and allegory so as to convey its critique of the prevailing social order in a strikingly realist while nonetheless dramatic fashion. Yet perhaps most crucially, the film's political aesthetic draws attention to the possibility of a radicalized pan-Arab commitment to the Palestinian struggle—across national and conventional borders.

Chapter Three focuses on the Egyptian-French co-production *Bab al-Shams* [*Gate of the Sun*] (2004), which, like *The Dupes*, blurs the boundaries of strictly national cinematic production. The film's transnational enabling conditions recall, critically, the Egyptian economy's opening to global capital under Nasser's successor, Anwar El Sadat, whose neoliberal *infitah* (open door) policies from the 1970s onward led ultimately to the dismantling of Egyptian socialist policy of the 1960s. The *infitah* laid the foundations for, and would continue throughout, the subsequent Mubarak era (1981–2011), during which *Gate of the Sun* was produced. Its production also broadly coincided with a number of other, decisive political events, perhaps most importantly Egypt's sudden move toward an ostensible "peace agreement" with Israel via the 1978 Camp David Accords—and, later, the 1995 Oslo II Accords, which in many ways sealed a future that further disenfranchised Palestinians and hindered the possibility of their self-determination. Under Sadat, the Egyptian state would align itself advantageously with the Israel–U.S.–Saudi Arabia bloc on political, economic and ideological grounds, setting the tone for a more conciliatory approach toward Israel, to the detriment of the Palestinians who continued to be marginalized and fragmented through various exilic and diasporic circumstances.

Despite these critical developments, a strong sense of popular commitment toward Palestine remained within the public consciousness and was roundly expressed in Egyptian leftist circles, which openly refused the state's normalizing tactics. This chapter focuses precisely on this problematic by posing the question of how emerging transnational production conditions presented Egyptian filmmakers with the option of either sanctioning the neoliberal status quo or advocating for social issues which challenge it, like the Palestinian struggle. Based on Lebanese author Elias Khoury's eponymous novel, the two-part epic drama was directed by one of Egypt's most prominent contemporary auteurs, Yousry Nasrallah, who typically seeks to diverge from commercial filmmaking. In contrast to the earlier, industry melodramas, which reference events in Palestine only tangentially, *Gate of the Sun* dedicates itself entirely to the telling of Palestinian history from within Palestine and its exilic diaspora and, in so doing, promotes solidarity with Palestinians in their struggle for justice. To these ends, *Gate of the Sun* deploys a range of aesthetic techniques, such as the frame story and oral histories, which together create a collective and counter-hegemonic Palestinian subjectivity. The film centers around Palestinians who were expelled from their Galilean villages at the hands of Zionist militias, and who were compelled to relocate to squalid refugee camps in Lebanon, where they and their progeny still live in an enforced state of limbo, waiting to return.

The analysis of a range of films in this book is intended to generate critical thought about the enduring, yet constantly changing relationship between politics and aesthetics across differing historical moments in the Egyptian cinematic involvement in the Palestinian struggle. The analyses stand to illustrate the challenges of representing an increasingly multigenerational and geographically multi-sited struggle that is also always subject to the precarity of global capitalism. Indeed, the *cinematic* text lends itself particularly well to interrogating and representing the Palestinian struggle and the intersecting questions, for it has the capacity to critique the status quo via both different political aesthetics and generic conventions and their interaction. Egyptian cinema has undoubtedly played its part in certain of these respects and therefore deserves to be taken seriously as both a meaningful cultural occasion for analysis and critique and a crucial source of historical documentation that gestures to Egypt's intimate relationship to Palestine across the twentieth century and until today.

Notes

1 As Toufic Haddad puts it:

> While the reality to unfold between Palestinians and Israelis as a consequence of the Oslo Accords and subsequent agreements failed to realize these expectations, ultimately leading to a situation where unprecedented levels of political violence became an all too familiar norm, the Israeli–Palestinian "peace process" nonetheless remains a resilient discursive and political framework in which the conflict is discussed in world media, and between the political leaderships of both sides (Haddad, *Palestine Ltd.: Neoliberalism and Nationalism in the Occupied Territory* (London: I.B. Tauris, 2016), 1).

For additional, legal background to this issue, see Noura Erakat, *Justice for Some: Law and the Question of Palestine* (Stanford, CA: Stanford University Press, 2020).

2 The Israeli occupation has its origins in the colonial Sykes-Picot (1916) agreement, which split the entire Fertile Crescent (modern Iraq, Syria, Lebanon, and Palestine) into French and British areas of direct influence. For more on this history, see Avi Shlaim, *The Politics of Partition: King Abdullah, the Zionists and Palestine 1921–1951* (New York: Columbia University Press, 1990), 24–6.

3 Benedict Anderson, *Imagined Communities: Reflections on the Origin and Spread of Nationalism* (London and New York: Verso, 1991). In his earlier work on the origins of nationalism, Anderson (1983) famously develops the notion of "imagined communities" and their construction and dissemination through media.

4 Terri Ginsberg, *Visualizing the Palestinian Struggle: Towards a Critical Analytic of Palestine Solidarity Film* (London: Palgrave Macmillan, 2016), 85.

5 As Edward Said alerts us, the Palestinian issue is often referred to incorrectly as a "conflict": "[T]here is no indifference, no objectivity, no neutrality because there is simply no room for them in a space that is as crowded and overdetermined as this one" (Said, "The Burdens of

Interpretation and the Question of Palestine," *Journal of Palestine Studies* 16, no. 1 (1986): 30). For him, the balanced logic of "conflict" insufficiently describes the substance of popular struggle, which assumes an asymmetrical rather than an even playing field.

6 As Yezid Sayigh argues:

> There is a *symbiotic* relationship between the Arab states and the Palestine question: the Palestinians are Arabs and share close ties of kinship, commerce and political history with their immediate neighbors; two million of them live in the Arab countries; Palestine has strong political and religious significance for all Arabs; consequently there is considerable overlap at the social, economic, and political levels between the refugee community and host population in each Arab county. This has led to widespread grassroots support among the Arab peoples, and even within various Arab armies, for the contemporary Palestinian national movement (Sayigh, "The Politics of Palestinian Exile," *Third World Quarterly* 9, no. 1 (1987): 38).

7 Ewan Stein, *Representing Israel in Modern Egypt: Ideas, Intellectuals and Foreign Policy from Nasser to Mubarak* (London: Bloomsbury Academic, 2012), 120.

8 See Adam Hanieh, *Lineages of Revolt: Issues of Contemporary Capitalism in the Middle East* (Chicago: Haymarket, 2013); Ali Kadri, *The Unmaking of Arab Socialism* (New York: Anthem Press, 2016); Hazem Kandil, *Soldiers, Spies, and Statesmen: Egypt's Road To Revolt* (London and New York: Verso, 2014); Sean F. McMahon, *Crisis and Class War in Egypt: Social Reproduction, Factional Realignments and the Global Political Economy* (London: Zed, 2017).

9 See Hanieh ibid.; Kadri ibid; McMahon ibid.

10 McMahon ibid., 17.

11 See Kandil, *Soldiers*; and Salem, *Anticolonial Afterlives*.

12 Oroub El-Abed, *Unprotected: Palestinians in Egypt since 1948* (Washington, ON: Institute for Palestine Studies; International Development Research Centre, 2009). This book offers a helpful resource for understanding not only the history of Palestinians in Egypt but the status of Palestinian refugees in one of several Arab host states (besides Jordan, Lebanon and Syria).

13 Yousef Yousef, *Qadiyat Filastin Fi Al-Sinima al-'Arabiyyah* (Beirut: Al-Muassasah al-'Arabiyyah li-al-Dirasat wa al-Nashr, 1980); and Bashar Ibrahim, *Filastin Fi Al-Sinima al-'Arabiyyah* (Damascus: Wezarat al-Thaqafah, 2005). Both of these works trace a historical trajectory that is similar to the one pursued in this book and confirm the relevance of the films selected for analysis here. While each provides a useful and much-needed historical overview, however, neither offers a deep-structural analysis of film aesthetics.

14 Numerous scholarly texts on Egyptian and on Palestinian cinema have referenced the films that are central to the present book, yet they hardly engage in textual analysis or articulate film aesthetics to the political-economic conditions underpinning the Egypt–Palestine relationship. Such texts include: Soraya Antonius, "The Palestine Cause in the Cinema," *Journal of Palestine Studies* 7, no. 2 (January 1978): 120–5; Qussai Samak, "The Arab Cinema and the National Question: From the Trivial to the Sacrosanct," *Cineaste* 9, no. 3 (1979): 32–4; and Joseph Massad, "The Weapon of Culture: Cinema in the Palestinian Liberation Struggle," in *Dreams of a Nation: On Palestinian Cinema*, ed. Hamid Dabashi (London: Verso, 2006), 32–44.

15 Ella Shohat, *Israeli Cinema: East/West and the Politics of Representation*, 2nd ed. (London and New York: I.B. Tauris, 2010), 13.

16 Ghada Hashem Talhami, *Palestine in the Egyptian Press: From Al-Ahram to Al-Ahali* (Lanham: Lexington Books, 2007), xi.

17 See also William Haddad, *The Arab–Israeli Conflict in the Arab Press: The First Three Decades* (London: Intellect Books, 2018).

18 Talhami, *Palestine in the Egyptian Press*, 347. See also Haddad ibid.

19 Shohat, *Israeli Cinema*, 251.

20 See Leila Ahmed, *A Border Passage: From Cairo to America—A Woman's Journey* (New York: Penguin, 2012); Radwa Ashour, *The Woman from Tantoura: A Palestinian Novel* (Oxford, UK: Oxford University Press, 2014); and Ahdaf Soueif, *In the Eye of the Sun* (New York: Knopf Doubleday, 2011). Arabic literature represents an interesting entry point in its own right, with the above authors being but three prominent Egyptian authors who wrote about Palestine in their literary work. See also Noha Radwan, "Palestine in Egyptian Colloquial Poetry," *Journal of Palestine Studies* 40, no. 4 (July 2011): 61–77.

21 Werner Ende concentrates on the post-1948 period to examine "some of the most important themes of this literature" (Ende, "The Palestine Conflict as Reflected in Contemporary Arabic Literature," in *The Contemporary Middle Eastern Scene: Basic Issues and Major Trends*, eds. Gustav Stein and Udo Steinbach (Opladen: Leske und Budrich, 1979), 157).

22 Joseph Massad, "Liberating Songs: Palestine Put to Music," *Journal of Palestine Studies* 32, no. 3 (April 2003): 21.

23 Kay Dickinson, "'I Have One Daughter and That Is Egyptian Cinema': `Azīza Amīr amid the Histories and Geographies of National Allegory," *Camera Obscura: Feminism, Culture, and Media Studies* 22, no. 1 (2007): 141.

See also Fredric Jameson, *The Political Unconscious: Narrative as a Socially Symbolic Act* (Ithaca, NY: Cornell University Press, 1981). Jameson's theory of allegory has been an important node of dialogue and debate in cinema and cultural studies for the way in which it conceives of cultural texts as "cognitive maps" of social and economic conditions of possibility. See also his "Third-World Literature in the Era of Multinational Capitalism," *Social Text* 15 (1986): 65–88; and "Cognitive Mapping," in *Marxism and the Interpretation of Culture*, eds. Cary Nelson and Lawrence Grossberg (Urbana-Champaign and Chicago: University of Illinois Press), 347–360.

24 Dalia Said Mostafa, *The Egyptian Military in Popular Culture* (London: Palgrave Macmillan, 2017).

25 Viola Shafik, *Popular Egyptian Cinema: Gender, Class, and Nation* (Oxford, UK: Oxford University Press, 2007).

26 Lina Khatib, *Filming the Modern Middle East: Politics in the Cinemas of Hollywood and the Arab World* (London: I.B. Tauris, 2006).

27 According to Khatib, "In their representations of the Arab–Israeli conflict, the American, Egyptian, and Syrian films engage in a similar discourse of difference, and advocate subjective nationalisms that form part of an on-going cultural battle over the same "homeland" and that complicate the mythical form of the nation" (ibid. 105). See also Shafik, *Popular Egyptian Cinema*.

28 Olivia C. Harrison, *Transcolonial Maghreb: Imagining Palestine in the Era of Decolonization* (Stanford, CA: Stanford University Press, 2015), 3.

29 Ibid., 4. See also John Martin Collins, *Global Palestine* (London: Hurst, 2011). Collins argues that we must situate "the local struggle over Palestine in relation to a series of global processes that continue to shape the conditions within which all of us live our lives" (2).

30 Harrison ibid., 69.

31 A number of shorter, focused monographs have also been published in recent years, such as Kay Dickinson's *Arab Film and Video Manifestos: Forty-Five Years of the Moving Image Amid Revolution*

(Cham, Switzerland: Palgrave Macmillan, 2018), which considers the politically potent form of the cinematic manifesto (including examples relevant to Palestine), and auteur studies such as Victoria Brittain's *Love and Resistance in the Films of Mai Masri* (Cham, Switzerland: Palgrave Macmillan, 2021) and Terri Ginsberg's *Films of Arab Loutfi and Heiny Srour: Studies in Palestine Solidarity Cinema* (Cham, Switzerland: Palgrave Macmillan, 2021).

32 Ginsberg, *Visualizing the Palestinian Struggle*. For a study on the possibility of transnational solidarity between Black radical thought and Palestine activism, see Greg Burris, *The Palestinian Idea: Film, Media, and the Radical Imagination* (Philadelphia: Temple University Press, 2019).

33 Nadia G. Yaqub, *Palestinian Cinema in the Days of Revolution* (Austin: University of Texas Press, 2018).

34 Kay Dickinson, *Arab Cinema Travels: Transnational Syria, Palestine, Dubai and Beyond* (London: British Film Institute, 2016).

35 For instance, the popular Arabic online magazine, *Romman*, similarly lists the early films discussed here: *A Girl from Palestine*, *Land of Heroes*, *Land of Peace*, *God Is with Us*, *Shadows on the Other Side*, *Nagi el-Ali*, and *Bab el-Shams*. See Amro Ashour, "Filastin fi al-aflam al-masriyya mundhu 1948 hatta bab el-shams," *Magallat romman al-thaqafiyah*, https://rommanmag.com/view/posts/postDetails?id=4407.

36 Joel S. Gordon. *Revolutionary Melodrama: Popular Film and Civic Identity in Nasser's Egypt* (Chicago: Middle East Documentation Center, 2002).

CHAPTER ONE

The Emergence of Palestine in the Egyptian Melodrama

The 1948 Palestinian Nakba, and the 1952 Free Officers coup that ushered in the republic of Egypt were two of the most transformative political events to take place in the Arab region during the mid-twentieth century. Not only would these events distinctively tie together the respective trajectories of Egypt and Palestine, but they also carried regional and global reverberations within the early Cold War period as it conditioned an ensuing emergence of postcolonial nation-states across much of the formerly colonized world. While Egyptian public awareness of Zionist colonial settlement in Palestine predated this period by at least two decades—whether among secular nationalists, members of the Muslim Brotherhood, within Egyptian communist circles or women's unions—it was in the years directly leading up to the 1952 coup, when popular grievances against British domination were on the rise, and Egypt's nascent military ruling class was establishing its legitimacy, that Palestine became an important mobilizing force and a symbolic national issue that would make its way into a variety of Egyptian media, including commercial film melodramas.

Attitudes toward the Zionist project to create a Jewish state on colonized Palestinian land were politically and ideologically uneven and sometimes divergent during Egypt's "liberal age"[1] (1923–52), with the Egyptian and Arab press effectively resembling a "battleground"[2] and the subject of Palestine becoming a veritable microcosm of the challenges facing the artificially divided yet socially, politically, and religiously plural Arab world under colonial rule.[3] The emerging Free Officers' movement, which gained momentum in the wake of the Arab armies' defeat against Zionism in the 1948 Palestine War, was able to capitalize on shared anti-colonial aspirations across political factions and the wider public, and subsumed them under its banner of nationalism once it came to power in 1952. Prior to that, the liberal Wafd party had spearheaded Egypt's growing nationalist movement (1919–52). The nascent postcolonial military regime, whose domestic and regional hegemony would endure across subsequent administrations,[4] set the stage for Egypt's initially pragmatic stance on the question of Palestine, with professed national interests—especially in ridding itself of British colonial presence—shaping most of its policy decisions in the early 1950s.[5] As one of Egypt's primary cultural sectors, cinema was integral to this critical moment of transition and revolutionary ferment. Its main output, the melodrama, has historically been perceived as a particularly favored cinematic genre precisely during times of political transition and ideological struggle—not least across national borders—whether because of its ability to respond to and comment upon change, or in its capacity to mediate attendant anxieties about subject formation and relations of difference such as class, gender and ethnicity. In the case of Egypt—where military defeat in the Palestine War was followed by a tumultuous transition from a colonially backed monarchy to an independent military regime—the relationship between the political and economic interests of the emerging nation-state and the needs and aspirations of ordinary people would assume a complex and at times contradictory dynamic that entailed an intricate negotiation between more overt measures of coercion and subtler strategies of creating consent. Partly for this reason, in addition to their commercial mass appeal, Egyptian melodramas of the period lend themselves well to closer scrutiny of the ideological practices framing early Egypt–Palestine relations.

The first two Egyptian feature films to reference Palestine, Mahmoud Zulficar's *Fatat min Falastin* [*A Girl from Palestine*] (1948) and Fatin Abdel Wahab's *Nadia* (1949) are both based on screenplays by Egyptian writer Yousef Gohar and involve Zulficar's wife, Egyptian actress Aziza Amir (as co-writer in *Fatat*, and as actress in *Nadia*). These two melodramas paved the way for a further three paradigmatic melodramas that were released after the 1952 coup: Niazi Mostafa's *Ard al-Abtal* [*Land of Heroes*] (1953), Ahmad Badrakhan's *Allah Ma'na* [*God Is with Us*] (1955) and Kamal el-Sheikh's *Ard al-Salam* [*Land of Peace*] (1957) are in many ways representative of this transitional period which also represents a watershed in Egypt–Palestine relations. Viewed as a set, these five films not only share thematic, narrative and formal tendencies with respect to Palestine, they also exemplify the contemporary state of Egyptian popular cinema in its melodramatic tradition, whether with respect to cinematic form—they are still steeped in the generic conventions established during the monarchical-colonial period and draw upon local theatrical practices—or in terms of their mode of production—they are still financially backed by the private sector even while evidencing a gradual turn to more explicitly anti-colonial themes.

On the level of plot, these films are characterized by a simple love story between an Egyptian military officer and, with the exceptions of *Nadia* and *God Is with Us*, a Palestinian woman. (Egyptian women in *Nadia* and *God Is with Us* also signify Palestine, however, typically through their waiting longingly for a brother's or lover's return). These romances, which usually culminate in marriage, either evoke the political climate preceding the Free Officers' coup or, in the later films, represent its direct incitement. Besides *Land of Peace*, which depicts a slightly later period, all of them revolve around Egypt's participation in the 1948 Palestine War, but as typical melodramas of the period, they work allegorically to disguise the serious politics of that involvement by projecting middle-class values onto highly mediated depictions. Familial and domestic concerns take center stage, with the Palestine War becoming the backdrop, whereupon familial interactions, emotional conflicts, and romantic relationships—and the various sites in which they play out—become readable as microcosms of middle-class Egypt during the war and the lead-up to 1952. Joel Gordon (2001) suggests that *God Is with Us* in fact allegorizes "an emergent official Free Officer history."[6]

By drawing attention to the overdetermined inscription of Palestine in these familial constellations, this chapter contributes a further analytical dimension to the Egyptian war melodrama against its transitional politico-historical context. Rather than excuse such films as mere propaganda and/or entertainment—although they were undoubtedly made with that function in mind—this set of films invites us to look "beneath the surface," to critically analyze the workings of melodrama in all of its ideological complexity. Taking this more layered approach to the popular genre enables us to see how Palestine figures allegorically through manipulative narrative-compositional structuring, patriarchal characterologies, and other melodramatic conventions such as tendentious musical motifs and carefully composed mise-en-scène, all of which contribute to the films' mass cultural appeal. For melodramas, while always products and "reproducers" of particularized realities, are also always excessive, projecting multiple, oftentimes didactic meanings. It is in the production of this excess that both the threat of ideological cooptation and, in turn, the possibility of its subversion are at once broached and contained. Indeed, in order for these films to fulfil the dual functions of producing commercial entertainment value and manufacturing consent for the emerging anti-colonial nationalist project, they make strategic use of the popular genre's narrative devices, generic conventions and stylistic features—in ways that have historically appealed to broad, commercial audiences.

Yet critical theories of melodramatic spectatorship, while recognizing the genre's pathos and affective appeal, draw attention to the importance of considering the observable totality of the cinematic structures in which the represented characters (inter)act in relation to "the operation of social and psychic forces they cannot control."[7] On such a view, we are compelled to read these early cinematic representations of Palestine as effective enablers of a heroic patriarchal trajectory through injury and defeat to ultimate betterment, and to articulate that trajectory to the rhetorical centrality of Palestine, and the Palestine War's constitutive role, in the Free Officers' ascent to power also depicted in the films. Such an allegorical reading of these nationalist texts opens analysis onto the intersecting sociopolitical and economic struggles underpinning what Gordon (1992) has called the "formative period of the Nasserist revolution."[8] For while nationalist calls for an independent Egypt, and mobilization of military support for Palestine will have managed to unify a broad, heterogenous base around a shared stake in ending colonialism, the emerging postcolonial state also worked to contain potential challenges to its rule. In the case of cinema, we see the deferral of symbolic attention to marginalized groups (women, peasants, urban poor), prescribing them idealized and stereotypified roles rather than addressing the political-economic structures that sustain their subjugation. In fact, these social groups, which would eventually be subsumed under the military leadership, were already forming unions and civil society movements in the decades leading up to 1952. By recognizing melodramatic complexity and laying bare the systemic social relations overdetermining their conventional meanings, we can grasp the significantly more complex and multifaceted historical determinants of the films' representation of the Palestine War and of Egypt's engagement therein.

It is precisely this critical relationality that we must consider when examining how this series of Egyptian war melodramas represents Palestine, for the Palestinian issue cannot be disentangled from the Egyptian struggle for independence—even though Egyptian anti-colonialism did in fact champion other struggles that were staked alternatively in Palestine liberation during the lead-up to the 1952 coup and the transition from monarchy to postcolonial nation-state. The post-World War Two period, for instance, saw an increase in mass politics, in which organizations of differing ideological bent, such as Islamist, communist, trade unionist, radical Wafd, and women's unionist competed for a say in the political arena.[9]

In short, by placing the Egyptian national interest at their narrative forefront, the films discussed in the present chapter marginalize the politically more complex circumstances framing the 1948 Palestine War/Nakba and the violent establishment of the Zionist state of Israel, drawing almost exclusive attention to Egypt's perceived stake and priorities vis-à-vis that geopolitical configuration. Thus these films inevitably render a limited understanding of the Palestinian issue in its contemporary totality, both in terms of the asymmetrical conflict entailed by the Nakba and the scale of the human and social catastrophe it produced, and symptomatize the emergent military state which, in its effort to rid Egypt of colonialism, came nonetheless also to engage in a suppression of dissenting positionalities that, given their manifest support for the Palestinian struggle, may otherwise have portended a different future for Egypt and its relationship to Palestine.[10]

Early Egypt–Palestine Relations: The Ideological Hegemony of Nationalism

The cluster of melodramas discussed in this chapter were all produced in the aftermath of the Nakba or, as Egypt and other Arab states that participated militarily commonly refer to it, the Palestine War. Corresponding to their order of production and the Free Officers' rise to power, the earlier two films produced before 1952, *A Girl from Palestine* and *Nadia*, are symptomatic of the conditions preceding the military coup, whereas *Land of Heroes* and *God Is with Us* that were produced in the wake of 1952, appropriately celebrate heroic military sacrifice en route to independence. The last of the set, *Land of Peace*, was not released until 1957, by which point Free Officer member Gamal Abdel Nasser had assumed the Egyptian presidency, and anti-colonial nationalism in Egypt was morphing more explicitly into a distinct form of pan-Arab nationalism, commonly referred to as Nasserism.

These films thus imply a connection between the Palestine War, in which the Egyptian regular army, comprised of volunteers spanning the political spectrum, was defeated by nascent Israel, and a surge in anti-colonial nationalism in Egypt that precipitated the Free Officer-led revolution. A chronological link between these two events, however, while historically accurate, obscures a more complex story. The Free Officers, who successfully toppled King Farouk's monarchy and seized power in 1952, had formed in pre-revolutionary Egypt out of a group of rising middle-class and nationalist officers, amongst whom were Nasser and several other key figures including Anwar El Sadat, his successor as President.[11] The group was by no means an ideological monolith or devoid of internal disagreement—the early power struggle that ensued between the first two Egyptian presidents,

Mohammed Naguib and Gamal Abdel Nasser, being a case in point.[12] Comprising a coalition of factions from across the political spectrum, including the liberal nationalist Wafd party, the right-wing nationalist Misr al-Fatat (Young Egypt) party, the Muslim Brotherhood, and members of the Communist movement, the Free Officers were able momentarily to put their differences aside and convene around growing anti-colonial sentiment and the shared goal of national liberation. It was particularly the officers' shared experience participating in the Palestine War, though, that clinched this supersession of ideological differences.[13] A causal link is therefore often drawn between the young army officers' battlefield experiences and their revolutionary actions upon return to Egypt, with military defeat in Palestine understood as the political lynchpin.[14] As Nasser's "Memoirs of the First Palestine War" explains, "I returned to my battalion in a state of revolt against everything. I was in revolt against the fact that it was by sheer accident that we had escaped catastrophe."[15]

Egypt was one of five neighboring Arab countries alongside Transjordan, Syria, Lebanon and Iraq which in mid-1948 sent a regular army to participate in the second phase of the Palestine War.[16] While Zionist mythology heroically refers to this war, which ended in Israeli victory, as the "War of Independence," Palestinians as well as other Arabs and their allies use the term Nakba, which more accurately accounts for the tragedy, still ongoing, that befell the Palestinian people. This Arabic term for "catastrophe" also connotes the comprehensive defeat of the Arab armies that occurred as a result of Israeli aggression and those armies' own limitations: "long lines of communication, the absence of reliable intelligence about their enemy, poor leadership, poor coordination, and very poor planning for the campaign that lay ahead of them."[17] These latter may be attributed in large part to European colonialism's divisive drawing of boundaries between previously interconnected Arab populations, including those settled in the Fertile Crescent. Colonial divisions notwithstanding, evidence of solidarity between Palestinians and neighboring Arab peoples is ripe if one looks at the "unofficial" first phase of the war, during which Palestinian irregulars were assisted by approximately 4,000 Arab volunteers comprising the Arab Liberation Army.[18] In the case of Egypt, a militant solidarity movement had already spread widely by the late 1930s, which—in advocating for sending volunteers to Palestine—stressed the need for a people's war that would connect the Egyptian and the Palestinian struggles.[19]

That "unofficial" first phase had erupted as a militant response to the 1947 United Nations "Partition Plan," which pronounced the division of Mandate Palestine into unevenly apportioned Palestinian and Jewish states and fomented the gradual, rapidly escalating violent displacement of more than half of historic Palestine's 1.5 million population—more than 750,000 Palestinian Arabs—from their lands and properties.[20] The majority of displaced Palestinians were forced to settle in refugee camps in neighboring "host" states,[21] while a remaining minority was rendered internally displaced inside the new Israeli entity. A significant number of Palestinian refugees settled in the Gaza Strip bordering Egypt, where they became subjects of Egyptian military administration from 1949–67.[22] Egypt had taken control of the Gaza Strip in 1949 as part of a strategy of making military and political concessions to Israel, primarily in order to prevent Transjordan from territorial advancement and consequent border sharing with Egypt.[23] The Palestinian diaspora would, in its formation, soon come to replicate the regional and class divisions characteristic of Palestine's pre-1948 reality. Whereas urbanized, middle-class refugees tended to settle in cities across the Arab region, the proletarian and peasant classes (*fellaheen*) as well as the *Bedouin* were usually confined to harsher conditions in the refugee camps set up after 1948 in Lebanon, Jordan and Syria.[24]

Egypt's precise motives for sending an army into Palestine have been subject to debate. Scholars have offered contesting views on Egypt's role in the war and provide differing reasons for its participation, which depend upon whether one is considering domestic politics, foreign policy or Egyptian public opinion, all of which were agitated and rapidly changing at the time.[25] The typical explanation for the monarchy's having sent troops into Palestine is King Farouk's purported struggle for prestige and regional control as against rival King Abdullah of Transjordan, who also had designs on Palestine.[26] Analysis of this controversial move has since shown the lack of genuine concern it revealed on the part of the monarchy for Palestinian rights.[27] A further critique of Egyptian military participation holds the ruling elite responsible for using the Palestine War as a diversionary tactic distracting attention away from bleak domestic social conditions.[28] This critique resonates with the faction-ridden Egyptian communist movement's view of what its constituents understood as bourgeois-nationalist complicity in the political-economic status quo at the expense of proletarian internationalism.[29] The regional rivalries evidenced by these explanations—again a legacy of imperial divide-and-rule—often hindered collaborative action and was exacerbated by the fact that national independence, not broader revolution-building, was a political priority for the Arab countries participating in the war.[30]

The Egyptian officers, who are portrayed prototypically in several of the selected melodramas, were wary of their military's unpreparedness and weakness in comparison with the Zionist paramilitary forces, or Haganah (which would evolve into the Israeli Defense Forces (IDF) following the formation of the Israeli state). As a result, they blamed Egypt's defeat on the undeniably corrupt monarchy, yet subsequently exploited that very loss in order to legitimize their own military rule. To this end, the officers directed a popular accusation against the monarchy—one emphatically foregrounded in several of the melodramas—which claimed that the king had backstabbed the military by providing it with defective weapons.[31] Nasser's *Falsafat al-Thawra* (*Philosophy of the Revolution*) (1954) exemplifies this militarist rhetoric. It insists upon a unified commitment to the need for military build-up and the participation of the Egyptian army in the Palestinian liberation struggle as a means to overthrow the monarchy and end British colonial rule:

> The situation needed a coherent power whose members are brought together within one framework, and who are not involved, to an extent, in individual or class conflicts (…) It was rather the development of events which defined for the army its role in the colossal struggle to liberate the nation.[32]

Revisionist historians have compared the emergent Free Officers' narrative to official Arab historiography, which similarly "discredited the old order by way of legitimizing militarism in the Arab world."[33] Likewise, the melodramas discussed here center military nationalist narratives, whereupon it is unsurprising that counter-hegemonic responses are marginalized if not completely absent from them.

Egyptian popular awareness of the Palestinian issue can be traced to the 1936–1939 Great Arab Revolt against the British Mandate in Palestine, when the Egyptian press reported on the events, and Egypt became something of an anti-Zionist hub.[34] In this context, the question of Palestine started to become of central concern to a range of Egyptian political and social movements, not least those which posed a challenge to the liberal nationalism represented by the local bourgeoisie who played a formative role in early Egyptian cinema. Conceiving of the Palestinian issue as simultaneously an Arab and a Muslim cause, Egypt's Muslim Brotherhood, which had emerged in the 1920s, spearheaded Egyptian efforts to assist Palestine in the Great Revolt.[35] Egyptian Muslims perceived Zionism as a threat to important Islamic sites in Palestine such as the Al-Aqsa Mosque in Jerusalem and thus understandably identified with Palestinians in opposition to the Zionist conquest of Arab land.[36] When the situation escalated during the 1948 war, the Muslim Brotherhood urged direct intervention and offered assistance to their Palestinian brothers.[37] For Egyptian communists, whose movement was born out of expanding Arab trade unionism in the early 1920s, Zionism first and foremost represented a reactionary nationalist movement dominated by the Jewish bourgeoisie of European origins.[38] In their belief, a global socialist revolution adhering to Marxism-Leninism as embodied by the newly formed USSR would not only solve the Palestinian—and Jewish—question, but could also end other forms of exploitation. The leftist movement was relatively unified on the Palestinian issue and rejected Zionism, colonialism and partition until the promulgation of the

1947 UN "Partition Plan," which the Egyptian communists—following the line of the Soviet Union—endorsed, to the dismay of Arab nationalists.[39] Thereafter, the movement progressively splintered and was faced with a "strong wave of popular condemnation."[40] Despite their contradictions, which include coalescing into military alliance during the Officers' coup, these two Egyptian responses to the Palestinian question, along with the aspiring and quite visible women's movement, are worth bearing in mind as possible challenges and alternatives to the hegemonic narratives presented in the selected films.

By the early 1950s, the Free Officers galvanized a wide spectrum of the Egyptian population under the banner of anti-colonial nationalism, but this new regime would ultimately not overhaul existing class relations, for the new military elite was clearly invested in maintaining the middle-class.[41] Egyptian Marxist scholar Anouar Abdel-Malek (1968) emphasizes structural continuities over a radical break during the lengthier transition from the colonial to the postcolonial Egyptian state through the 1950s–60s, noting how the new regime's "military-technocratic elite," which monopolized the state apparatus and its varied ideological institutions (such as mass media and the arts), would persist on the basis of a state capitalist formation.[42] Similarly, another Egyptian Marxist, Mahmoud Hussein (1973), notes that the state apparatus which the Free Officers inherited from the Palace in 1952, was "designed to prevent any popular initiative" and thus gave them the advantage of "achiev[ing] power within the framework of the established relations of production."[43] Drawing upon the ideas of Frantz Fanon, who stresses the risks underpinning the transition from a colonial to a postcolonial order, Sara Salem (2020) explains how the emerging Egyptian state never managed to untether itself wholly from the "colonial international,"[44] since it excluded the working classes from any decision-making power.[45] Not only might this proletarian left, had it not been weakened, possibly have contributed to a more radical restructuring of the postcolonial state, it might also have "resisted the neoliberalization to come in the 1970s."[46] In hindsight, we can only speculate whether and how a more empowered Egyptian left might have confronted the Palestinian issue under the new republic. Egypt's ongoing ties to the colonial international, and the fact of a new shared border delimiting the Zionist military threat, prevented the Egyptian state from adopting a bolder position on Palestine. As Rosemary Sayigh (2007) has argued:

> The same social and political weaknesses that made the Arab states incapable of intervening effectively in Palestine in 1948 have made them unwilling to support fully the struggle to liberate Palestine since then, even though Israel's predominance also threatens their vital national interests.[47]

Whatever their political orientation, the different stances on Palestine in pre-1952 Egypt are testament to the complex, contradictory and ideologically overdetermined nature of the situation. Egypt's "early moderation vis-à-vis Israel"[48] and ultimate recognition of Zionist statehood is in fact concealed within much of the official rhetoric and remains absent or obscured in the selected, pro-military melodramas. Following its defeat in the Palestine War, in 1949 Egypt accepted a UN proposal, which Israel also signed—an agreement which "formally terminated the state of belligerency" between the two states.[49] The Free Officers are known to have corresponded with the United States before the 1952 coup, with U.S. President Franklin Delano Roosevelt reportedly stating that the Egyptian military would be a necessary force for modernizing the new state in ways "agreeable to the West without causing too much turmoil."[50]

In the end, although Egypt's defeat in Palestine was a galvanizing factor for the 1952 revolution, the new republic's stance and policies pertaining to the Palestinian issue would see no major change in the early post-revolutionary years.[51] As much as this moment was heralded as foundational in Egypt—and, as this book argues, marked a concomitant emergence of the Palestinian issue in Egyptian cinema—many economic and governing practices carried over from the monarchical to the republican period, not least the repression of groups already working in solidarity with Palestinians, that might have offered other and additional forms of support for their struggle and been more radically committed to ending and "delinking" from the larger global configurations that had originally wrought both British and Zionist colonization.[52]

Foundations of the Egyptian Film Industry and the "Revolutionary Melodrama"

The first Egyptian films to reference Palestine were produced toward the end of Egypt's liberal era, following the Free Officers' military participation in the Palestine War and in the context of the anti-colonial nationalism which this experience catalyzed. While the Palestinian issue had already entered the field of contesting anti-colonial discourse from the 1930s, it was only in the wake of the Israeli national establishment in 1948 that the subject was first addressed cinematically, in *A Girl from Palestine*. A series of similar melodramas would follow in subsequent years, all produced by Egypt's private-sector film industry, the foundational commercial structures of which were already in place by the 1930s.[53] While cinematic representations of Palestine and Palestinians originate at "the dawn of the moving image, with both the Lumiere Bros. and Edison companies filming in Ottoman Palestine by the late nineteenth century,"[54] early Arab filmmaking about Palestine was in fact limited to Egypt, insofar as Egypt was the first and only Arab country with an established film industry before the 1960s.[55] Financed by Egyptian nationalist entrepreneur Tala'at Harb's Bank Misr, the prolific Studio Misr—which produced *Land of Heroes*, *God Is with Us*, and *Land of Peace*—was founded in 1934 as part of an effort by the nascent national bourgeoisie to achieve economic independence from the British.[56] While the revolutionary moment around 1952 produced a lineage of directors who would later contribute to Egypt's public-sector cinema in the 1960s, the Hollywood-like industry within which Egyptian cinema grew up persisted through the 1950s. As such, with production remaining in the hands of the private sector, the nationalist melodramas still adhered primarily to commercial market factors.[57] Prominent features of commercial Egyptian cinema—to this day—are its flourishing star system and its affinity for genre films such as comedies, musicals, and melodramas. Perhaps more so than Hollywood, these features have placed Egyptian cinema into a transnational mode of production along with the Indian and Mexican—and, much more recently, Nigerian—cinemas, which are also thriving entertainment industries with a penchant for music, dance, humor and drama. As in these industrial cinemas, the successful star actors and actresses of early Egyptian film frequently collaborated with the same producers, directors and scriptwriters across successive projects. The director of *God Is with Us*, Ahmed Badrakhan, for instance, worked with prominent Egyptian singer Umm Kulthoum on numerous productions after returning from his studies in Paris. Niazi Mostafa, who directed *Land of Heroes*, started out as an important promotional documentary filmmaker for the Misr Group during the mid-1930s before producing a prolific number of films that repeatedly featured the crème de la crème of Egyptian stars—for example, Naguib el-Rihani, Kouka (whom Mostafa married), Anwar Wagdi and Aziza Amir. Women played an important role in the formation and development of the Egyptian film industry, with *A Girl from Palestine* and *Nadia*, the first two Egyptian films about Palestine, both produced by actress and producer Aziza Amir's company, Aziza Amir Films, in the late 1940s.[58] The career of *Nadia*'s director Fatin Abdel Wahab, who went on to make 52 films between 1949 and 1970, testifies to the scale of production in which many of these Egyptian filmmakers were involved. And like other transnational film industries, Egyptian private-sector cinema—although part of Bank Misr's efforts to "Egyptianize" the industry—was rarely singularly Egyptian-run, with the liberal nationalist business class interacting both with local foreign and international capitalist investors to finance film production.[59]

This transitional period of Egyptian filmmaking had a tremendous impact on conventional genre cinema, with new themes emerging and heroic narratives cultivated in the years surrounding the 1952 coup. According to Gordon (1999), despite the limitations of the 1952 revolution, a number of taboo-breaking films were released in the years to follow "that treated issues of social class and social justice (…) even if some continued to incorporate song and dance and melodramatic tropes."[60] Although it took several years to establish, the new government encouraged Egyptian directors to create more revolutionary anti-colonial films and, in this way, develop a "self-conscious national film industry."[61] Unsurprisingly, Egypt's emergent ruling military class not only sought to consolidate and lead a sovereign, postcolonial state but understood the didactic value of cinema and became interested in exploiting it as a "political tool to enhance their ideology and glorify the military regime in power."[62] The question of ideology in the context of this transitional period—soon to become a salient feature in post-1952 intellectual life—raises the issue of censorship, which was officially expanded to include cinema in 1904 and administered by the Ministry of the Interior.[63] In 1947, the Ministry of Social Affairs introduced a newer version of this law which for the first time prohibited "scenes that could encourage disruption of the social order, such as revolutions, demonstrations or strikes."[64] This law remained in place until Nasser came to power, after which, in 1955, the Ministry of Public Information eliminated all previous censorship regulations and replaced them with Law 430.[65] Much like Hollywood's Hays Code, these Egyptian ordinances comprised "prohibitions related to social mores and morals" as well as to matters of "national security and public safety" such as "expressions of popular mass dissent."[66] Privileging conventional genre fare, the censors especially scrutinized films that criticized the monarchy or state authority.[67] *God Is with Us* was one such "taboo-breaking" film that, while reflecting the official narrative of the "revolutionists," initially failed to clear censorship and was not screened until 1955, despite its having already been publicized two years earlier.[68]

Gordon's (2000) theory of "revolutionary melodrama" enhances our understanding of the genre, by gesturing to the unstable conditions underpinning the revolutionary moment that are symptomatized by this particular censorial tendency at a moment in which earlier censorship laws were in fact being eased.[69] These critical attributes usefully inflect the commonsense, apolitical, entertainment-driven conception of melodrama within aesthetic-historical context, alluding to the vast social changes that swept across Egypt during the period. Characteristically, these "revolutionary" and proto-"realist" films dramatize events preceding and producing the revolution. This veritable historical rehearsal involved representation of the

Palestine War as a formative event and symbolical instrument of nationalist sentiment, at once staking broad commercial appeal and legitimating emergent Free Officer leadership.

As mentioned, scholars diverge when it comes to defining the precise meaning and function of melodrama. Suffice it here to say that the cinematic melodrama derives its basic generic parameters and conventions from a theatrical and literary tradition, wherein exaggeration—of plot, character, affect and style—is perhaps the most prominent trait. Melodramatic narratives construct meaning through hyperbolic devices and binary oppositions, often positioning the figure of the victim into conflict with her counterpart, the hero, to form a matrix of subjective identification. Melodramas typically promote such identification by evoking feelings of empathy, pity, fear, and suspense. Songs and music play a particularly meaningful role in this construction ("melos," after all, means "melody" or "musical"), with musical sequences—especially throughout Egyptian cinema's first "Golden Age" (1930s–50s)—constituting a central and particularly popular element. Massad (2003), writing in another context, makes the relevant point that, in comparison to other artistic forms, such as literature, poetry, plays and painting, it is songs about Palestine and the Nakba which were most popular and "probably reached the largest number of people."[70] Music must therefore be acknowledged as particularly critical and instructive in the selected melodramas, especially since several of the songs featured in them are about Palestine or are performed by Palestinians.

Framing Palestine and Plotting the Emergence of the Egyptian National Hero

As cinematic analogies to the rise to national power and importance of the Free Officers against the backdrop of the Palestine War, *Land of Heroes* (1953) and *God Is with Us* (1955), each produced by Studio Misr, narrate the trajectory of emerging national heroes. While varying in content and contextual focus, their narrative turning points are offset—and their melodramatic features enhanced—by the young officers' encounters with Palestine as a site of conflict and romance. The films are set during the period leading directly to the 1952 coup, whereas *Land of Peace*, released several years later in 1957, focuses on Egyptian soldiers collaborating with Palestinian *fedayeen* against Zionist military operations along the borders of the Gaza Strip (a likely intertextual reference to the Israeli raid on Gaza in 1955), by which time Nasser had become President of Egypt. Set in the earlier climate of the Palestine War, the two forerunners to this trio, *A Girl from*

Palestine and *Nadia*, both produced by Aziza Amir Films, are more visibly centered around female characters: Palestinian refugee Salma, who falls in love with an Egyptian pilot in *A Girl from Palestine*, and Egyptian orphan Nadia, whose brother is martyred in the war, and who subsequently finds comfort in a romantic relationship with an Egyptian officer.

The narrative temporality of these melodramas is structured to provide a sense of immediacy and urgency, possibly because most of them were produced in the wake of the 1948 war, and is thus not particularly self-reflexive, instead culminating in national heroic telos. They arguably fall under what Walter Armbrust (2000), referring to Egyptian cinema between 1945–52, calls a "cinema of war profiteers": a fast-paced, profit-driven production trend characteristic of the post-World War Two period several years prior to Gamal Abdel Nasser's rise to power.[71] In this respect, they exemplify the tendency of melodramas to mediate historical processes of rupture, political transition and ideological struggle, just as they can be understood as instrumental to national subject formation. What shall be outlined here, then, through a closer look at their plots, narrative structures and stylistic devices, is the particular role Palestine assumes and enacts in these emerging, melodramatically excessive, war narratives.

Land of Heroes and *God Is with Us* both feature young Egyptian officers who are compelled to volunteer to help their "Arab brothers" in Palestine by joining the military, and in so doing also believe they are fulfilling their patriotic duty to adopt the masculine role of protecting budding Egypt from external threats and enemies.[72] Particularly illustrative of this cultivation of proactive military subjectivity in the context of transforming Egypt into a sovereign state are numerous disciplinary military training sequences. In *Land of Heroes*, the army is actually described as a "madrasat al-rogola" (school of manhood). Adel (Gamal Fares), a typical young, middle-class officer, falls in love with a Palestinian woman during his military stint in Palestine. He meets Azza (Kouka[73]) while on a leisurely stroll through a Palestinian market (possibly in Gaza,[74] as her name also evokes), and she invites him to her home along with some of his comrades. Charmed by this romantic encounter, Adel pleads that Azza return with him to Egypt for marriage and a shared future—the last scene depicts them with a son. This ending echoes that of *A Girl from Palestine*, in which Salma also marries an Egyptian officer named Adel back in Egypt. *God Is with Us* similarly involves a romantic plot strand. In this rendition, the young officer-protagonist Ahmad (Imad Hamdi[75]) returns to Egypt from the Palestine War, which has evoked in him a revolutionary spirit played out by his insistent yearning for Nadia (Faten Hamama[76]), his supportive cousin and fiancée who has faithfully awaited his return—and possibly references Aziza Amir's Nadia. *Land of Peace*, the first Egyptian film set entirely in Palestine and featuring a majority of Palestinian characters (albeit played by Egyptian actors), likewise depicts a blossoming love story between an Egyptian officer, Ahmad (Omar Sharif) and Palestinian woman, Salma (again Hamama), who encounter one another when Salma is asked to care for his injuries incurred in a military operation carried out against the Zionists, which Ahmad's military comrades did not survive.

In *Land of Heroes* and *God Is with Us*, the young officers' returns from Palestine are accompanied by physical impairments, to which their female counterparts respectively tend, and which trigger confrontational scenes with their elders, whose suspected secretive dealings with defective weapons are deemed responsible for the injuries and Egypt's loss of the war. *Land of Heroes*' key scenes of conflict play out between protagonist Adel and his father (Abbas Fares), who is revealed to have been involved in exporting faulty weapons to the army, with the unfortunate side-effect of their having caused his son's injuries. When Adel exposes his father as corrupt at the end of the film, the latter, humiliated, commits suicide. In her allusion to these early Egyptian representations of Palestine, Nadia Yaqub (2018) suggests that such films indicate how "alienated or dissolute young men either learn to redeem themselves through political engagement or end their lives in a spectacular, depoliticized martyrdom."[77] Indeed, in all of these films, the male protagonists make physical sacrifice in the name of nationhood. A variation of the defective weapons theme occurs in *God Is with Us*, in which protagonist Ahmad's uncle, who is also his future father-in-law, is part of the corrupt network accused

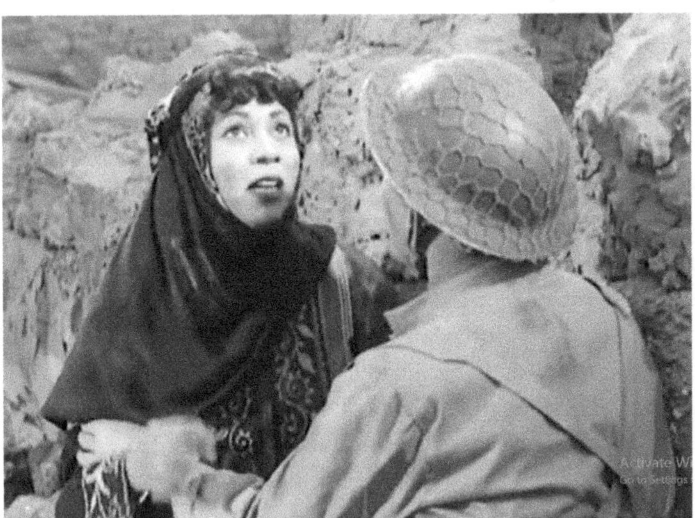

Figure 1.1 *A Girl from Palestine* [*Fatat min Falastin*] (Mahmoud Zulficar, Egypt, 1948).

of having contributed to the conditions which led Ahmad to lose his arm in battle. Attention is then directed to the officers conspiring to topple the monarchy after the war. As Dalia Mostafa (2016) suggests in her work on the representation of the military in Egyptian popular culture, such scenes depict "how the Free Officers' movement gained momentum."[78] The screenplay for *God Is with Us* was written, not coincidentally, by Ihsan Abdel Quddous, a prolific novelist and journalist for several Egyptian newspapers including *al-Ahram* and the popular political magazine, *Rose el-Youssef* (later nationalized by Nasser), whose investigations into the weapons scandal, and fiery critique of the royal palace led to his brief imprisonment under King Farouk,[79] and many of whose literary works position women as sacrificial symbols expected in that capacity to participate in public life—an emerging tendency also marking these cinematic melodramas.

In effect, *Land of Heroes* and *God Is with Us* both emphatically communicate the widely circulated nationalist indictment of the corrupt monarchy and its supporting elite for purportedly having insufficiently prepared the Egyptian military for the Palestine War. Not only are these melodramas infused with the emergent Free Officers rhetoric which, in criticizing the monarchy, sought to legitimate the nascent regime's political power, but they may anticipate what was to come several years later in the form of Nasserism.[80] And while the injuries sustained by the protagonists of these films may be read as embodied evidence of Egypt's defeat in the war, and thus, by extension, as allegories of a grander narrative of loss with respect to that defeat's effects on Egypt, they also function as convenient pretexts for developing the fictional romances which in turn indicate an underlying relationality between Egypt and Palestine. In this respect, the films all permit their protagonists to regain health and strength. Each narrative ends with conciliatory, forward-looking scenes: in *Land of Heroes*, with procreation between the Egyptian protagonist and his Palestinian wife; in *God Is with Us*, with the Free Officers revolution; and in *Land of Peace*, with the protagonist's return from a successful guerilla operation. (Ahmad, sympathetically referred to in *Land of Peace* as "al-gareeh al-Masry" (the injured Egyptian), regains his strength in a bed provided by Salma's family in their Palestinian village). The narrative redemption of these losses in turn enables a centering of Egypt's national predicament and consequent determination for liberation from colonialism, while deferring the unresolved complexities of that struggle onto the war's more acutely affected population, the stateless Palestinians. In so doing, these films evade genuine engagement with the Palestinian struggle and deeper critique of the political-economic Egyptian status quo.

Indeed, Palestine in this cluster of early 1950s war melodramas stands as a topical and symbolic backdrop for the lighthearted emplotment and favorable resolution of the Egyptian drama, supplying spectatorial pleasure in the Egyptian male subject's romantic encounters in Palestine and/or Egypt. This fetishistic construction of Palestine is underscored by the opening sequences, which set up the heroic narratives, both visually and aurally. *A Girl from Palestine* presents a triumphant series of Arab flags, presumably denoting the armies participating in the war, while *Nadia* opens "In a Village in Palestine," as per an introductory intertitle, and *Land of Heroes* begins with a silhouette of a soldier, a gun poised at his hip and pointing toward the sky. An enlarged, handwritten Arabic script is then superimposed onto this image, over which a triumphant male voice-over introduces the film by thanking "the heroes, who guard our borders, and who ensure the peace of our (home)land." After the sound of a cannon, the film title is pronounced by the same voice and projected onto the screen, followed by an intertitle reading "Cairo 1946" (an interim year that will later be emphasized by a 1948–52 calendar montage at film's end). In this way, the nationalist discourse is introduced, the plural "our" summoning an implied subjectivity to embark upon the ensuing narrative journey. While *Land of Heroes* endorses this subjectivity as patriotic identity, an allegorical elaboration connects it, and the "land" it interpellates, to the Palestinian struggle, not least since the film's central conflict revolves around *Palestinian* territory in the face of Zionist invasion. In *God Is with Us*, the initial credits are projected over a stereotypical orientalist backdrop: an image of a pyramid next to one of a minaret. A subsequent cut to war footage appears to capture, as the voice-over reveals, the events of 1948. Into this scenario a map of Palestine is blended, on which the names of several towns and villages are identified. The voice-over introduces the Palestine War as a "holy war which the sons of Egypt set out to join, and in which they endured horrors, faced fire and death." A subsequent claim states that Egypt was defeated as a result of a conspiracy "hatched against the nation" by *al-taghiyya* (the tyrant). Although this tyrant remains unnamed, the implication is clearly Farouk, who is dethroned by film's end. *Nadia* begins with a typically didactic classroom scene, where Egyptian teacher Nadia—whose brother we learn was killed in the Palestine War—gives a "Muhadara 'an Falastin" (lecture on Palestine) to a room full of female pupils. Her lecture is aided by a map of Palestine, drawn on the blackboard, which underscores its instructive and geographical significance and serves to visualize the otherwise imagined place.

While tangentially about Palestine (that is to say, the Egyptian officers' participation in the Palestine War), apropos of Thomas Elsaesser's dialectical theory of melodramatic excess as contained by techniques of mise-en-scène, this introductory didactic scene both constructs and illustrates the ideological banner under which nationalist rhetoric was being framed and fostered.[81] To that end, it bears noting that Nadia's lesson is proudly praised by an officer, who stresses the importance of her educational work for the nation—a rehearsal of emergent discourses on the importance of women's labor and civic participation that would be institutionalized under state feminist policies in the subsequent decade.[82]

The films' nationalist dissimulations of Palestine are also underscored by the representation of newspapers and other media in scenes in which the didacticism of media and the propagation of nationalist ideology are explicitly foregrounded. Following a scene in *Land of Heroes* in which Adel is portrayed as distressed after having walked in on his father flirting with Adel's own love interest, an elliptical cut occurs to a garage in which car mechanics are at work. Adel steps into the scene and is greeted by news headlines. One of the mechanics turns to him and asks, "*Hadretak* (Sir), did you not read the newspaper today?" Adel, at this point still portrayed as disengaged from politics, dismisses him and sweeps the newspaper aside, answering, "I don't read the news!" After Adel climbs into his car, the worker reiterates, urging the visibly feckless Adel to heed the call for Egyptians to volunteer for war, that "the situation is bad in Palestine." An insert shot of the headlines reads: "The Egyptians have set off to volunteer in the war," thus quickly framing Palestine as a news alert and illustrating the popular call being disseminated at the time by the media to the Egyptian working and middle classes. (In *Nadia*, his mediated call for Egyptian support extends to and implicates women, as Nadia learns that the army needs nurses. In *A Girl from Palestine*, furthermore, a group of women is shown gasping and rejoicing in exaggerated unity in response to news headlines concerning the war.) With the events in Palestine rendered as urgent news, in *Land of Heroes* the young officer Adel is visibly mobilized to volunteer. The brief news scene thus figures as a significant narrative turning point with a didactic undertone, in which the war in Palestine calls for an Egyptian response. Yet a further elaboration of the causes and conditions of the war and the interests of its political stakeholders remains absent. Not long after reading the headlines, Adel tells his parents he wants to join the army, proclaiming: "It is our duty." The emotionally charged directness of his statement fosters audience identification with Adel while gesturing to the class tensions underpinning the film's thematic conflict between personal choice and social obligation; Adel's words instructively allegorize the middle-class base of the Free Officers regime.

The fact that Adel had not initially heard the news about Palestine is also allegorical. After a brief shot of a pensive Adel, dramatic music sets in as the ensuing sequence shows him gazing at a portrait of his mother before packing it in his suitcase in preparation for joining the armed forces. Although the unfolding Palestine War is headlined as a means of jolting the protagonist into action, *Land*

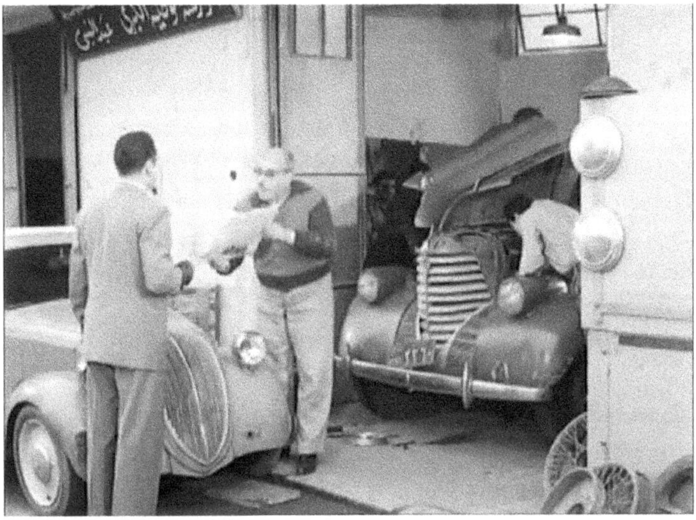

Figure 1.2 *Land of Heroes* [*Ard al-Abtal*] (Niazi Mostafa, Egypt, 1953).

of Heroes does not present an explanation or even pose the question of why the war is happening. There is no mention of Israel, let alone of the war's effects on Palestinians. At most, apropos of Yaqub's (2018) claim that "fictional features of Egyptian commercial cinema (...) failed to address Palestinian concerns,"[83] the film projects a generic enemy for the purposes of creating drama and suspense within the plot. In so doing, *Land of Heroes* illustrates the fabrication of a hegemonic Egyptian discourse on Palestine—one in which the primary anti-colonial goal of overthrowing the monarchy relegates Palestine to the periphery—as well as draws attention to a parallel history of Palestinian representation in the Egyptian mass media. According to Talhami (2007), the Egyptian press was "obsessed with the Palestine question in response to popular agitation and desire for news."[84] Yet the press at that time was far more diverse intellectually than the commercially managed film industry, boasting pro-government newspapers, a feminist press, religious media and other papers.[85]

God Is with Us includes similarly illustrative scenes regarding the importance of media to public information concerning the Palestine War. Referencing more explicitly the group of conspiring young officers attempting to take control of the newspapers from their previous owners, the *kubbar* (ancien régime; *lit.* adults), *God Is with Us* shows them strategizing how best to disseminate information to the public. While the Palestine War figures as a central concern, the issue of the corrupt weapons scandal once again circumvents any explanation of the war's causes and its real effects on Palestinians. In one exemplary scene, the officers are seated at a round table in a darkened room, the limited overhead lighting suggesting utmost privacy. As the officers take turns speaking, the camera closes in on their individual faces, and through this alternation presents the respective voices as a collective subject of which the protagonist Ahmad is arguably the narrative figurehead. During the discussion of the corrupt weapons scandal, one of the officers exclaims, "the people don't ever have an idea about anything!" This statement, mired in middle-class bias, initiates a debate about the usefulness of the newspaper as a means of reaching the masses, the final consensus being that it is "the only way." Scenes such as this symptomatize the fact that *God Is with Us* is not really about Palestine or solidarity with it. Instead, the officers want to use the newspapers in order to blow the cover on the *Egyptian* monarchical authorities' alleged sabotage of the Palestine War which in this film, too, is an allegory for the *Egyptian* rather than Palestinian liberation struggle. As marketed commodities then, these industry melodramas aimed to celebrate the formation of a sovereign Egypt for a new national subjectivity teetering within the contradictions of a militarized middle-class. Their closed, linear narratives and unequivocal messages were composed to mediate the trajectory of nascent Egyptian heroes, whereupon the significance of the Palestinian struggle for the liberation of Egypt from its contradictions—which would have entailed *genuine* support for the Palestinian struggle and an explicit rejection of Zionism—is overshadowed by an emphasis on Egyptian self-determination. As Ginsberg (2016) puts it, these Egyptian melodramas "project serious politics indirectly or (…) deploy political themes, mainly of heroism and sacrifice, especially regarding Palestine, as ideological means of distracting attention from domestic problems and their structural relationship to the Zionist entity."[86] In fact, the films make no distinction between the positions taken by the various contemporary political parties toward Zionism or the perpetration of the Nakba. Predating the discourse of normalization by at least thirty years, the films' representations of Zionism figure it simply as a generic threat to national security. Again, while this may satisfy on the level of entertainment, it cultivates a limited ideological understanding of the Palestinian issue that persists within Egypt to this day.

Melodramatic Excess: Gendered Allegories and the Function of Music

While Egyptian participation in the Palestine War in these films allegorizes an emergent Egyptian nationalism, Palestine emerges as a gendered allegory both through female characterologies and the element of music. According to Dickinson (2007) regarding national allegory in Egyptian cinema, "allegory is one of the most detailed, solid, and narrative forms of nonliteral expression, the one best suited, perhaps, to an understanding of meaningful yet fictional creatures like film characters."[87] In view of the proliferation of gendered, classed and racialized characters in popular Egyptian cinema of the post-World War Two period, I contend here that Palestine is represented in the selected melodramas as a feminized counterpart of the proto-nationalist Egyptian subjectivity which these films interpellate.

As noted, the central male characters in the films bear uncanny resemblance to the Egyptian Free Officers in terms of their middle-class status, military pursuits and patriotic rhetoric. Their heroic trajectories in fact structure the filmic narratives; they are the prisms through which depictions of Palestine must be understood. In *Land of Heroes*, for instance, the officers refer to Azza as the "Arab girl from Gaza," despite her insistence that she be referred to by her village identity, *al-Majdaliyya* (from al-Majdal in historic Palestine). The officers' usage of "Arab" here may serve as a unifying identity marker against the shared Zionist enemy–playfully acted out by two boys in *Land of Peace*: ("What do you want to play? Arabs and Zionists!")—but, by the same token, it indexes an early sense of Egyptian pan-Arabism: "Ya Salma, is that an Arab like us? Yes. From Egypt." On the level of dialect, the Egyptian soldiers and the Palestinians they encounter repeatedly, often comically, act out vernacular particularities: Azza's "shoo, shoo, shoo?" draws attention to the Palestinian dialect, whereas the culinary terms *falafel* and *ta'ameya* are emphatically distinguished as, respectively, Palestinian and Egyptian. This vernacular mode of identification is replicated by the encoding of the Palestinian woman Azza as a rural villager (Kouka, the Egyptian actress playing her is known for her Bedu roles)—a tactic that differentiates the Egyptian protagonist-officers as urban and middle-class. The correlation between nationality, class and dialect is also performed in household dialogues between servant and patron, placing the Palestinian and Egyptian peasant struggles on a similar plane, although by the end of the film, Azza—having married Adel in Egypt—is dressed in fancy, urban garb. Although seemingly overshadowed by the Egyptian officers' heroic participation in the Palestine War, the films' female characters (mothers, sisters, lovers) help advance the respective narratives by serving as emotional support for their male counterparts in pursuit of nationalist goals. They are unlike the fathers or fathers-in-law, whose greedy talk and intergenerational conflicts associate them with the corrupt ancien regime. Egyptian mothers, following conventions of melodrama during this period, are portrayed as selfless, endorsing their sons' patriotic actions unconditionally.[88] They typically

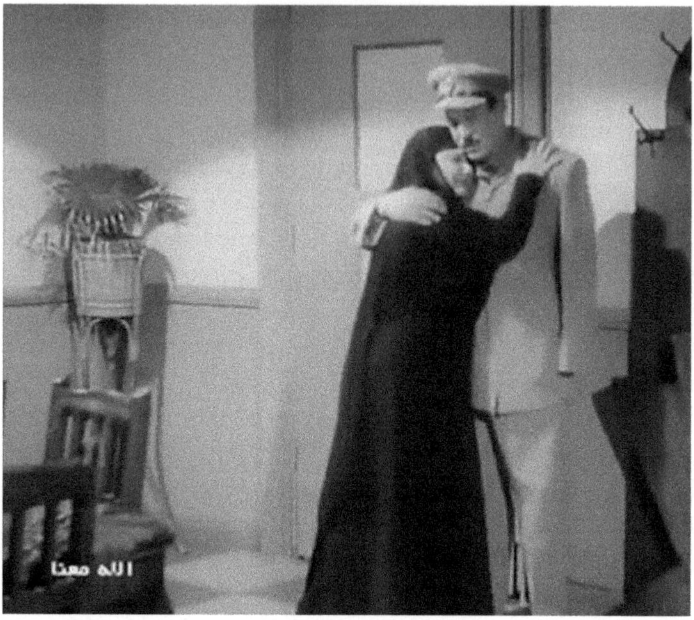

Figure 1.3 *God Is with Us* [*Allah Ma'ana*] (Ahmed Badrakhan, Egypt, 1955).

appear in emotional farewell and return scenes that punctuate the war melodramas, evoking maternal metaphors of home, nation and community. Their pronouncements tend to rehearse official-sounding, patriotic speech containing moralistic judgment or advice. In her analysis of women's films produced by Hollywood during World War II, Mary Ann Doane (1987) observes that the wartime absence of males created an excessive cinematic temporality marked by waiting and longing, which heightened melodramatic pathos while containing the possibility of a more sustained form of women's independence within middle-class limits.[89] This feminist reading of the genre foregrounds the female character and her melodramatic "function [as] excess and unresolved contradictions."[90] In the Egyptian melodramatic rendering of the Palestine War as a distant event for the women left behind, we find a similar phenomenon at work: scenes in entryways or at train stations mediating arrival and return and fostering a certain popular image of Palestine experienced as readily consumable by Egyptians. Emphasizing the separation from and return to mothers, in the opening scene of *Land of Peace*, Ahmad sits at the base of a tree, romantically reciting a letter to his mother in Egypt: "My dear mother, I'm not in Alexandria as I told you before I travelled. I'm in Palestine."

Christine Gledhill (1986) famously states that "melodrama is not about revolutionary change, but about struggles within the status quo."[91] This understanding prompts us to recognize these scenes of present-absent mothers, sisters and lovers as signifiers of struggle and subjugation within the "domestic" status quo of Egypt during the period of the Palestine War. *A Girl from Palestine*, *Land of Heroes* and *Land of Peace* all feature young Palestinian women with whom the Egyptian officer-protagonists fall in love and happily unite; the love stories in *Nadia* and *God Is with Us* involve Egyptian women waiting for family members to return from the war. These romantic narratives rehearse popular (mis)perceptions of Palestine while masking inconsistencies in Egyptian foreign policy toward its Palestinian neighbor. Palestinian refugees Salma (*A Girl from Palestine*) and Azza (*Land of Heroes*), for instance, are compelled, as a result of the war, to flee to Egypt. The opening scene of *A Girl from Palestine*, in which a chorus of women lyrically mourns the loss of Palestine ("Where are you coming from? Where are you going?" "Oh, Palestine we left crying for you") is exemplary of the way in which female flight from Palestine to Egypt allegorizes the Egyptian absorption of Palestinian refugees into Gaza in the wake of the Nakba. Azza's name (in its Arabic pronunciation) in fact repeatedly evokes the Gaza Strip, which was placed under Egyptian military administration from 1949 until 1967.[92] Such depictions underscore the films' propagation of postcolonial Egypt as an Arab patron of displaced Palestinians, a narrative that would be elaborated under Nasser during the mid-1950s.

This narrative of patronage is itself underscored by the way in which Palestinian women in these films are positioned as objects of male desire at the same time as they perform caretaker roles for Egyptian soldiers. Numerous hospital bed scenes in which injured soldiers are looked after by war nurses in Palestine stand as sites of maternal displacement and, as such, further the rehearsal of patriotic rhetoric ("for the sake of our nation," "sacrifice," etc.). Allowing for requisite moments of dramatic intimacy, such scenes posit nurses as indispensable to the well-being of the Egyptian officers and, by implication, the health of the Egyptian nation.

Perhaps the most compelling melodramatic conventions for both the representation of Palestine and the dissemination of nationalist ideology in these Egyptian war melodramas are the musical sequences that punctuate them. Indeed, music in general and songs in particular have, throughout Egyptian cinema history consistently served the dual function of appealing to a wide audience while cultivating and sustaining the star system. Arab national icons Umm Kulthoum, Abdel Halim Hafez and Mohammed Abdel-Wahhab all famously worked as singers and as actors—and sang songs about Palestine.[93] In the films analyzed here, Egyptian singer Souad Mohammed (1926–2011), who plays Salma in *A Girl from Palestine*, stands as a significant example of this popular phenomenon, as does the soundtrack's lyricist, Egyptian anti-colonial nationalist poet Bayram al-Tunisi (1893–1961). Souad sings multiple songs about Palestine in the film, and al-Tunisi's religiously inflected, anti-colonial lyrics underscore the film's mobilizing potential and general ideological direction. For instance, one of the film's title songs, *Ya Mujahid fi Sabil Allah* ("Oh Fighter for the Sake of Allah") laments the Palestinian tragedy, expresses a desire to return to Palestine, and summons the Arabs to go and defend Palestine. The fact that these lyrics speak to a broader Arab nationalist base as well as incorporate a religious audience suggests that these films opened up the possibility of fostering solidarity with Palestine across the political and religious spectrum, just as they simultaneously contain the threat of such ideological cooptation.

While the emphatically nationalistic songs in *A Girl from Palestine* clearly serve to underscore the film's hegemonic narratives, it is worth noting that the musical sequences in many of the films are often placed strategically in ways that appear to interrupt or deflect from serious dialogue about circumstances in Palestine. For instance, a scene in *Land of Peace* set up to ignite romance captures Palestinian Salma standing hesitantly between the front door and a table at which Egyptian soldier Ahmad is seated playing with her dress buttons. As her father's voice summons her from outside, Salma fearfully begins to tell Ahmad about her village's fear of another *tafteesh* (inspection). A brief close shot of Salma reinforces her point: "If you knew our conditions, you'd know why we're scared." However, as she proceeds to talk about the violence that has been inflicted on the village, Deir Yassin—site of one of the largest and most violent massacres of the Nakba[94]—the camera centers Ahmad (Omar Sharif), whose pensive face may visually distract attention away from the content of Salma's continuing speech about what happened to her mother and sister during the massacre. Later, when Ahmad announces, "I will take you back to Egypt," Salma's response that she would miss Palestine, her father, and Deir Yassin is superseded by music along with Ahmad's interjection that he wants children and for Salma to be their mother. Similarly in *Land of Heroes*, when the Egyptian officers are portrayed off-duty during the Palestine War, chatting to hospitable Palestinian Azza and her father over breakfast, an occasion is presented for explaining the current situation in Palestine. Ahmad asks Azza where she is from, to which she proudly responds "al-Majdal."[95] Yet rather than recount why she had to leave her village—that is to say, for the soldiers to hear about her family's expulsion from their home village by the Zionists—Azza's answer is turned into an occasion for celebrating Egyptian nationalism, which her father underscores in his expressed admiration for Egypt. The film then erupts into a three-minute song-and-dance scene in which Azza sings *al-Majdaliyya* (The Girl from al-Majdal), her predicament smoothly cloaked in song lyrics and relegated to the function of popular entertainment.

Thus by instrumentalizing Palestinian women and the backdrop of the Palestine War as means to entertain while also enabling and structuring the Egyptian hero's journey, these films evade a more contextualized treatment of the subject matter, one that might seriously have critiqued the Nakba and the settler-colonial state of Israel. At the same time, the popular musical soundtrack evokes a kind of "imagined community" (to borrow Benedict Anderson's term) that may address the spectator in its own right, by creating a spectatorial regime beyond what is central to the narrative—one that contains both the possibility for solidarity and the risk of cooptation.

We might therefore refer back to Doane's writings on the war melodrama, in which she points to the capacity of music and song to convey the "invisible"—"that which is just beyond the edge of the frame."[96] *Al-Majdaliyya* as well as Salma's repeatedly expressed desire to sing in *A Girl from Palestine* invite us to think about music as the medium through which Egyptian cinema channels and projects its imaginary of the Palestinian struggle. The films' representations of Palestine may seem on one level to resist the hegemonic framings discussed earlier on, which emerge as melodramatic excess. Paradoxically, however, it is precisely the melodramatic mode, commonly understood as conservative or trivial, that allows for this excess to appear and function affectively, beyond the narrative arc and alongside but beyond the emerging narrative of Free Officer nationalism. It is precisely these popular expressions that were able to captivate a broad audience through their construction of a shared sense of Egyptian nationhood and, with that, a shared imaginary of Palestine. Reading these first representations of Palestine in Egyptian cinema in this way prepares us for the next chapter, in which directors who came of age during this formative moment of anti-colonial nationalism and nascent Nasserism, would go on to make more explicitly political films in resistance to the political status quo and in increasingly radical solidarity with Palestine.

Notes

1 Fawaz A. Gerges, *Making the Arab World: Nasser, Qutb, and the Clash That Shaped the Middle East* (Princeton: Princeton University Press, 2018), 35–59.

2 Ghada Hashem Talhami, *Palestine in the Egyptian Press: From Al-Ahram to Al-Ahali* (Lanham, MD: Lexington, 2007), 5.

3 Tareq Y Ismael, *The Communist Movement in the Arab World* (London and New York: Routledge Curzon, 2005), 35.

4 Ziad Fahmy, *Ordinary Egyptians: Creating the Modern Nation Through Popular Culture* (Stanford, CA: Stanford University Press, 2011), 10. Citing the Italian scholar Antonio Gramsci's writings on hegemony, Ziad Fahmy describes how the establishment of nation-state hegemony entailed the creation of internal "others" (a kind of political regionalism), not only in Egypt but also in other national contexts such as Italy and the United States. Similarly, Sara Salem frames her study of modern Egypt (from the 1952 revolution to the 2011 revolution) by drawing upon Gramsci's concept of hegemony and the formation of "historical blocs" through a mix of coercion and consent (Salem, *Anticolonial Afterlives in Egypt: The Politics of Hegemony* (Cambridge, UK: Cambridge University Press, 2020)).

5 Yezid Sayigh, *Armed Struggle and the Search for State: The Palestinian National Movement, 1949–1993* (Oxford and New York: Oxford University Press, 1997), 12.

6 Joel Gordon, "Class-crossed Lovers: Popular Film and Social Change in Nasser's New Egypt," *Quarterly Review of Film and Video* 18, no. 4 (October 2001): 389.

7 Christine Gledhill, "Christine Gledhill on 'Stella Dallas' and Feminist Film Theory," *Cinema Journal* 25, no. 4 (1986): 46.

8 Joel Gordon, *Nasser's Blessed Movement: Egypt's Free Officers and the July Revolution* (New York: Oxford University Press, 1992), 4.

9 See Laura Bier, *Revolutionary Womanhood: Feminisms, Modernity, and the State in Nasser's Egypt* (Stanford, CA: Stanford University Press, 2011), 44.

10 The question of the presence/absence of dissenting positionalities within these nationalist films is of course a complex issue, to which further research might attend.

11 For further discussion of how the experiences of the 1930s and 1940s shaped the political trajectory of the Free Officers, see James P. Jankowski, *Nasser's Egypt, Arab Nationalism, and the United Arab Republic* (Boulder, CO: Lynne Rienner, 2002), 14.

12 In 1953 the Revolutionary Command Council (RCC) proclaimed Egypt a republic and appointed Mohammed Naguib as prime minister. In 1954 a crisis between two competing political traditions ensued: Naguib's liberal democratic approach and Nasser's emerging state capitalism.

13 Reem Abou-El-Fadl, *Foreign Policy as Nation Making: Turkey and Egypt in the Cold War* (Cambridge, UK: Cambridge University Press, 2018), 107. For a good overview of the different factions, see Anouar Abdel-Malek, *Egypt: Military Society: The Army Regime, the Left, and Social Change under Nasser*, trans. Charles Lam Markmann (New York: Random House, 1968), 18–28.

14 James P. Jankowski, *Nasser's Egypt, Arab Nationalism, and the United Arab Republic* (Lynne Rienner Publishers, 2002), 15.

15 Gamal Abdul Nasser and Walid Khalidi, "Nasser's Memoirs of the First Palestine War," *Journal of Palestine Studies* 2, no. 2 (1973): 27.

16 Avi Shlaim, *The Iron Wall: Israel and the Arab World* (New York: W. W. Norton, 2014), 34.

17 Avi Shlaim, "Israel and the Arab Coalition in 1948," in *The War for Palestine: Rewriting the History of 1948*, eds. Eugene L. Rogan and Avi Shlaim, 2nd ed. (Cambridge, UK: Cambridge University Press, 2007), 81.

18 Shlaim, "Israel and the Arab Coalition," 81.

19 Mahmoud Hussein, *Class Conflict in Egypt: 1945–1970* (New York and London: Monthly Review Press, 1973), 74. The nascent Egyptian feminist movement, another instance of early, organized pan-Arabism, also mobilized around Palestine liberation—and led to the gradual institutionalization of Arab feminism. See Margot Badran, *Feminists, Islam, and Nation: Gender and the Making of Modern Egypt* (Princeton, NJ: Princeton University Press, 1995), 223.

20 Rochelle Davis, *Palestinian Village Histories: Geographies of the Displaced* (Stanford, CA: Stanford University Press, 2010), 7.

21 Of the approximately 300,000 Palestinians who fled beyond Palestine's borders, 104,000 went to Lebanon, 110,000 fled to Transjordan, and 82,000 went to Syria. Some 12,000 went further afield to Iraq, Egypt, Libya, Saudi Arabia, even London. See Rosemary Sayigh, *Palestinians: From Peasants to Revolutionaries*, New ed. (London and New York: Zed, 2007), 100.

22 Oroub El-Abed, *Unprotected: Palestinians in Egypt since 1948* (Washington, ON: Institute for Palestine Studies / International Development Research Centre, 2009), 3.

23 Fawaz A. Gerges, "Egypt and the 1948 War: Internal Conflict and Regional Ambition," in *The War for Palestine: Rewriting the History of 1948*, eds. Eugene L. Rogan and Avi Shlaim, 2nd ed. (Cambridge, UK: Cambridge University Press, 2007), 167.

24 Sayigh, *Palestinians*, 101. Palestine's small, semi-sedentarized bedouin population shared the same conditions of poverty as the peasant class. By 1948, two-thirds of Palestine's Arab population was still rural. Sayigh, *Palestinians*, xxiv.

25 Thomas Mayer, "Egypt's 1948 Invasion of Palestine," *Middle Eastern Studies* 22, no. 1 (1986): 28.

26 Gerges, "Egypt and the 1948 War," 158.

27 Hazem Kandil, *Soldiers, Spies, and Statesmen: Egypt's Road To Revolt* (London and New York: Verso Books, 2014), 11.

28 Gerges, "Egypt and the 1948 War," 152.

29 Ismael, *The Communist Movement*, 33.

30 Gerges, "Egypt and the 1948 War," 151.

31 Ibid., 159–61.

32 Gamal Abdel Nasser, *Falsafat al-Thawra* (Cairo: Madbouli, 2005).

33 Gerges, "Egypt and the 1948 War," 160.

34 Jacob Abadi, "Egypt's Policy Towards Israel: The Impact of Foreign and Domestic Constraints," *Israel Affairs* 12, no. 1 (January 2006): 161.

35 Israel Gershoni, "The Muslim Brothers and the Arab Revolt in Palestine, 1936–39," *Middle Eastern Studies* 22, no. 3 (1986): 370.

36 Gerges, *Making the Arab World*, 68.

37 Michael Doran, *Pan-Arabism Before Nasser: Egyptian Power Politics and the Palestine Question* (Oxford, UK: Oxford University Press, 1999), 131–32.

38 Ismael, *The Communist Movement*, 2.

39 Ibid., 35.

40 Talhami, *Palestine in the Egyptian Press*, 67. See also Tareq Y. Ismael and Rifa'at El-Sa'id, *The Communist Movement in Egypt, 1920–1988* (Syracuse, NY: Syracuse University Press, 1990). Ismael lays out how, by the early 1950s, Haditu—which represented a culmination of the growing communist movement—had "experienced a resurgence amid the general political malaise following the Palestine war. It attracted members from all segments of society, including the demoralized Egyptian army, and had contacts with the free officers' movement. In fact, Haditu was the only political group that had organized branches in the military. Its membership increased to about 3000 by 1952" (69).

41 Hussein, *Class Conflict in Egypt*, 78.

42 Abdel-Malek, *Egypt: Military Society*, xix.

43 Hussein, *Class Conflict in Egypt*, 105, 87.

44 Samir Amin discusses how "Nasser wagered on industrialisation as the way out of the colonial international specialization which was confining the country in the role of cotton exporter. His system maintained a division of incomes that favoured the expanding middle classes without impoverishing the popular masses" (Amin, *The People's Spring: The Future of the Arab Revolution* (Pambuzuka Press, 2012), 19–20).

45 Salem, *Anticolonial Afterlives in Egypt*, 154.

46 Salem, *Anticolonial Afterlives in Egypt*, 101.

47 Rosemary Sayigh, *Palestinians: From Peasants to Revolutionaries*, New ed. (London and New York: Zed, 2007), 104.

48 Raymond William Baker, *Egypt's Uncertain Revolution under Nasser and Sadat* (Cambridge, MA: Harvard University Press, 1978), 35.

49 Gerges, "Egypt and the 1948 War," 167.

50 Kandil, *Soldiers*, 24. Here it is furthermore useful to distinguish between the British and U.S. role in the Arab region in the late 1940s and early 1950s, and in turn the onset of the Cold War. While the gradual eclipse of British imperialism was underway at this point, the more explicitly pro-Zionist United States was only just beginning to assert itself. For more, see Ray Takeyh, *The Origins of the Eisenhower Doctrine* (London: Palgrave Macmillan, 2000).

51 El-Abed, *Unprotected*, 40.

52 Prominent Egyptian Marxist, Samir Amin utilizes the notion of "delinking" to conceptualize how countries "at the periphery of the world-capitalist system" need to undergo a process of "delinking"—that is to say, the refusal to submit national-development strategy to the imperatives of "globalization." (Amin, "A Note on the Concept of Delinking." *Review (Fernand Braudel Center)* 10, no. 3 (1987): 435.)

53 Walter Armbrust, "Egyptian Cinema On Stage and Off," in *Off Stage/On Display: Intimacy and Ethnography in the Age of Public Culture*, ed. Andrew Shryock (Stanford, CA: Stanford University Press, 2004), 83.

54 Nick Denes, "Between Form and Function," *Middle East Journal of Culture and Communication* 7, no. 2 (2014): 221.

55 Nadia Yaqub, *Palestinian Cinema in the Days of Revolution* (Austin: University of Texas Press, 2018), 26.

56 Viola Shafik, *Popular Egyptian Cinema: Gender, Class, and Nation* (Cairo: American University in Cairo Press, 2007), 21.

57 Jane Gaffney, "The Egyptian Cinema: Industry and Art in a Changing Society," *Arab Studies Quarterly* 9, no. 1 (1987): 58.

58 Gaffney, "The Egyptian Cinema," 55.

59 Magdy Mounir El-Shammaa, *The National Imaginarium: A History of Egyptian Filmmaking* (Cairo: American University in Cairo Press, 2021), 29.

60 Joel Gordon, "Film, Fame, and Public Memory: Egyptian Biopics from Mustafa Kamil to Nasser 56," *International Journal of Middle East Studies* 31, no. 1 (1999): 64.

61 Ella Shohat, "Egypt: Cinema and Revolution," *Critical Arts* 2, no. 4 (January 1983): 22.

62 Dalia Said Mostafa, *The Egyptian Military in Popular Culture* (London: Palgrave Macmillan, 2017), 29.

63 Nehad Selaiha, "The Fire and the Frying Pan: Censorship and Performance in Egypt." *TDR* 57, no. 3 (2013): 21.

64 Malek Khouri, *The Arab National Project in Youssef Chahine's Cinema* (Cairo: American University in Cairo Press, 2010), 12.
65 Only in 1976 would these measures be amended to include new restrictions under the Sadat regime. See Khouri, *The Arab National Project*, 13.
66 Joel Gordon, *Revolutionary Melodrama: Popular Film and Civic Identity in Nasser's Egypt* (Chicago: Middle East Documentation Center, 2002), 59–60.
67 Schochat, "Egypt," 24.
68 Gordon, *Revolutionary Melodrama*, 69.
69 Shafik, *Popular Egyptian Cinema*, 108.
70 Joseph Massad, "Liberating Songs: Palestine Put to Music," *Journal of Palestine Studies* 32, no. 3 (April 1, 2003): 22.
71 Walter Armbrust, *Mass Mediations: New Approaches to Popular Culture in the Middle East and Beyond* (Berkeley and Los Angeles: University of California Press, 2000), 301.
72 This general dynamic similarly pervades Aziza Amir's "women's films," in which patriotic duty is expressed in the form of teaching, nursing and charitable actions.
73 Egyptian actress Kouka is best known for her portrayal of a Bedu character in several films, including *Antar bin Shaddad* [*Antar the Black Prince*] (1961), also directed by Niazi Mostafa.
74 As Yaqub explains in a brief section about early representations of Palestine in Egyptian cinema: "In these films, the Gaza Strip is a liminal space to which young Egyptian men travel to escape overbearing fathers or personal failure" (*Palestinian Cinema*, 26).
75 Egyptian actor Imad Hamdi also worked as an accountant and production/distribution manager for Studio Misr. Hamdi's last role was in the renowned new realist film *Sawwaq al-Utubis* [*The Bus Driver*] (Atef El Tayeb, 1982).
76 Faten Hamama is a prolific and respected Egyptian actress, if not one of *the* icons of Egyptian cinema. She starred in a number of films alongside Omar Sharif, and the two were married for a period.
77 Yaqub, *Palestinian Cinema*, 26.
78 Mostafa, *The Egyptian Military*, 28.
79 Iman Hamam, "Exceptions to the Rule: The Mechanics of War and the Institution in Egyptian Cinema," in *Cinema of the Arab World: Contemporary Directions in Theory and Practice*, eds. Terri Ginsberg and Chris Lippard (Cham, Switzerland: Palgrave Macmillan, 2020), 329. For further discussion of Ihsan Abdel Quddous, see Gordon, *Revolutionary Melodrama*, 134.
80 Mostafa makes this important connection when she suggests that these war melodramas offer a visualization of Nasser's published memoirs of the Palestine War (*The Egyptian Military*, 29).
81 Thomas Elsaesser, "Tales of Sound and Fury: Observations on the Family Melodrama," in *Imitations of Life*, ed. Marcia Landy (Detroit: Wayne State University Press), 68–92.
82 As Bier argues, "the state which emerged as a result of the 1952 revolution embodied both the promises and the limitations of the preceding half century of modernizing discourses on feminism, the nation, and inclusion" (*Revolutionary Womanhood*, 25).
83 Yaqub, *Palestinian Cinema*, 26.
84 Talhami, *Palestine in the Egyptian Press*, 347.
85 Ibid.
86 Terri Ginsberg, *Visualizing the Palestinian Struggle* (London: Palgrave Macmillan, 2016), 104.

87 Kay Dickinson, "'I Have One Daughter and That Is Egyptian Cinema': `Azīza Amīr amid the Histories and Geographies of National Allegory," *Camera Obscura: Feminism, Culture, and Media Studies* 22, no. 1 (2007): 140.

88 In a convention found in global melodrama of this period and earlier, mothers tend to figure as moral arbiters who are innately patriotic, whether due to their link to "traditional community" or the affective capacity that extends from love for their children to selfish love for their motherland. Both Maxim Gorky's 1906 novel, *Mother*, and Vsevolod Pudovkin's 1926 cinematic adaption of it are prototypes of this convention. Despite ultimately being positioned as corrupt wrongdoers and implicit targets of criticism, the fathers in these two films are not characterized as pure evil. Instead, their oftentimes comical behavior invites spectatorial identification and sympathy, thus affording them a more subtly ideological role.

89 Mary Ann Doane, *The Desire to Desire: The Woman's Film of the 1940s* (Bloomington: Indiana University Press, 1999), 179.

90 Laura Mulvey, *Fetishism and Curiosity* (Bloomington: Indiana University Press, 1996).

91 Gledhill, "Christine Gledhill," 45.

92 El-Abed, *Unprotected*, 3.

93 Muhammad Abdel-Wahhab's "Filastin," produced in 1949 is a paradigmatic example. For more on Palestine in Arab music, see Joseph Massad, "Liberating Songs: Palestine Put to Music," *Journal of Palestine Studies* 32, no. 3 (April 2003): 21–38.

94 The most notorious massacre of Palestinians during the Nakba took place in the village of Deir Yassin, where between 120 and 254 unarmed civilians were brutally murdered. See Nur Masalha, *The Politics of Denial: Israel and the Palestinian Refugee Problem* (London: Pluto Press, 2003), 32–45.

95 Al-Majdal was among the 418 villages that were "emptied" during the war and were "absorbed geographically into the new Israeli state" (Davis, *Palestinian Village Histories*, 9).

96 Doane, *The Desire to Desire*, 50. See also Gledhill, who similarly argues that melodrama "operates in the field of the known and familiar, but also attempts to short-circuit language to allow the 'beneath' or 'behind'—the unthinkable and repressed—to achieve material presence" ("Christine Gledhill," 45).

CHAPTER TWO

Resisting the Limits of Egyptian Cinema: Pan-Arab Representation of Palestine

Two decades after the 1952 Free Officers' coup, which set the stage for the nationalist presidency of Gamal Abdel Nasser, Egyptian director Tawfik Saleh produced the first feature-length film to focus expansively on the Palestinian struggle: *Al-Makhdu'un* [*The Dupes*] (1972). Based on Palestinian writer Ghassan Kanafani's novella *Rijal fi al-Shams* [*Men in the Sun*] (1962), and the product of a collaborative, pan-Arab effort to cinematically narrate the post-Nakba years, the critically acclaimed realist film is in several ways representative of self-critical discourse within the Arab region concerning the 1967 Naksa, known also as the Defeat. In the aftermath of the Six-Day War, the Zionist occupation of Palestine expanded into the West Bank and Gaza Strip (what together would become known as the Occupied Palestinian Territories) along with the Golan Heights / al-Jawlan in Syria and the Sinai Peninsula in Egypt—a crucial territorial asset Egypt would exchange for a peace treaty and normalizing trade relations with Israel in 1978.[1] *The Dupes* foreshadows the social, economic, and political enabling conditions of the Naksa that triggered the Palestinian shift to armed guerilla struggle as a liberatory strategy as against the previous state-sponsored military resistance efforts spearheaded by Egypt under Nasser. The film was awarded prizes at the Damascus International Film Festival and Carthage Film Festival (CFF) but was never shown publicly in Egypt. Its form and content as well as its conditions of production situate this politically committed film at a critical juncture in Arab cinema history, characterized by a surge in revolutionary fervor fomented by the further loss of Palestinian land. As Rasha Salti (2006) describes it, the emerging cinematic aesthetic "was not crafted to entertain, it was impelled by a duty to crystallize the aspirations of the people and to represent their struggles."[2]

The Naksa signaled the retreat of Nasserist pan-Arabism, of which the nationalization of the Suez Canal in 1956 as well as Egypt's short-lived unification with Syria in the form of the United Arab Republic (UAR) from 1958–61 were important components. Nasser's state socialist policies, which made the Egyptian public sector a key employer and engine of economic growth, extended to the establishment of the General Egyptian Institution for Cinema, Radio, and Television in 1963, following the first stirrings of a cinematic public sector as early as 1957.[3] This state-sponsored film industry would last until 1971, when it was partly re-privatized by Nasser's successor, Anwar El Sadat, who would assume the leadership of Egypt a couple of years before *The Dupes* was produced. Due to obstacles he faced within this sector, Tawfik Saleh traveled to Syria to produce *The Dupes* under the auspices of the Syrian National Film Organization (NFO). In Syria, the already prolific realist auteur was soon joined by other politically committed, anti-imperialist and pro-Palestine filmmakers from across the Arab region who sought to pursue an alternative, collective mode of production outside of Egypt and/or in collaboration with other Arab state funding entities.[4] *The Dupes* is one of the first in a series of post-Naksa Arab films whose production conditions stretch the boundaries of the national cinema framework and exemplify the more radical, intersectional and materialist version of pan-Arabism being practiced among Arab intellectuals and artists dissatisfied with its statist incarnations in the form of Nasserism and, in Syria and Iraq, Ba'thism.

Saleh's migration to Syria raises the question of Syria's (geo)political relationship to Egypt, especially regarding their political allegiances in the Cold War, and Syrian cinema's stake in the Palestinian issue following the dissolution of the UAR. An emerging counterweight to the regional domination of commercial Egyptian cinema,[5] the Syrian NFO was inaugurated in 1963 as a wing of the Syrian Ministry of Culture.[6] By the early 1970s, Damascus would become a hub for alternative Arab and Palestine solidarity filmmaking, with the NFO recruiting Arab filmmakers to collaborate on Syrian productions with a pan-Arab and/or Palestine solidarity bent. Arguably an extended form of Syrian state support for the Palestinian resistance movement, the NFO particularly encouraged the production of realist films about the Arab–Israeli struggle. As such, numerous documentaries were made, including Iraqi director and prolific film editor Qais al-Zubaidi's productions of *Ba'idan 'an al-Watan* [*Far from the Homeland*] (1969) and *Shahadat al-Filastinyyin fi Zaman al-Harb* [*Testimonies of Palestinians in the Time of War*] (1972), both about the harsh living conditions of children in Palestinian refugee camps.[7]

Under the broader Cold War conditions in which Syria cultivated not only military but cultural and educational ties with the Socialist Bloc dominated by the USSR, the Syrian public-sector mode of cinematic production—some of whose earliest output comprised foreign cooperations (such as the Ministry of Culture's first short film, *Sa'iq al-Shahinah* [*The Truck Driver*] (1966), directed by the Yugoslavian Boško Vučinić[8])—effectively came to institute a Soviet work ethic and labor practices.[9] In addition to structural similarities, socialist themes and aesthetic styles from the Soviet film tradition began making their way into Syrian cinema, appearing first in *The Dupes*, *Al-Fahd* [*The Leopard*] (Nabil Maleh) and *Al-Sikkin* [*The Knife*] (Khaled Hamadeh)—all released in 1972. This Soviet connection would become even more salient by the 1980s and into 1990s, when prominent Syrian auteurs like Mohammad Malas and Oussama Mohammed attended the renowned Gerasimov Institute of Cinematography (VGIK) in Moscow and, upon return to Syria, started making films that focused heavily on local issues, with a "strong emphasis on formalism, aesthetic composition and symbolism."[10]

In contrast to Egyptian war melodramas from the early 1950s, then, in which the Palestine War forms a backdrop for emergent Free Officer nationalism, and Palestinian women figure as a romanticized Other to Egyptian heroes, *The Dupes* offers a more critical perspective on the Palestinian issue that places Palestinians at the dramatic forefront, permitting them narrative agency and enabling them to become "the protagonists of their own story." Blending subjective techniques such as flashbacks and point-of-view shots with archival inserts of political events related to the Nakba, *The Dupes* presents a multi-perspectival cross-section of Palestinian exiles unified by a quest for material betterment that takes them to the Gulf states—an intertextual reference to the oil migration that would become common throughout the Arab region with the onset of neoliberalism. The film's symbolic rhetoric weaves an intricate critique of the prevailing sociopolitical and economic order, expressing mistrust of corrupt leaders and allegorizing—importantly by way of its ending—the turn to the autonomous armed resistance that would characterize the Palestinian struggle for decades to come.

The Implications of Nasserism for Palestine and Egyptian Cinema

Under the leadership of Nasser that spanned the mid-1950s and 1960s, a series of important events, agreements and global developments shaped the course of Egyptian politics and Egypt's involvement in the Palestinian struggle. The former

Free Officer received widespread recognition and rose to popular fame following his decision in 1956 to nationalize the Suez Canal Company, formerly owned by the British colonial power—a foundational step in a broader effort to decolonize the Egyptian economy. While this bold move triggered the second Arab–Israeli war (also known as the Suez Crisis)—when Britain, France and Israel colluded to seize and occupy the canal—their subsequent withdrawal under pressure from the United Nations, United States and Soviet Union effectively marked the end of direct foreign presence in Egypt and paved the way for Nasser's state-led economic development plan that placed the key means of production under public ownership.[11] Globally speaking, Nasserism instantiated the Keynesian period of the welfare state.

Nasser's state socialist policies included land reform, nationalization of property, and provision of food subsidies and access to public education, employment, and healthcare. These reforms substantially improved the living standards of Egypt's working and peasant classes while reducing rents and profits for the wealthier classes, thus creating an overall more equitable distribution of resources. Nonetheless, radical left critics of Nasserism expressed dissatisfaction, arguing that Nasser's conception of socialism was insufficiently anti-capitalist and driven by the Egyptian state bourgeoisie and military actors seeking control of the economy.[12] Indeed, Nasser's state socialist system did depend to a great extent on the removal of the working classes and left-wing forces from real decision-making power.[13] Although Nasserism's tangible benefits for the majority of Egyptians have been lauded, the Egyptian state evidently also suppressed resistance to its monopoly on power from the communist left, and imprisoned many members of the Muslim Brotherhood—following an assassination attempt on the president by a suspected member in 1954.[14] These tensions and contradictions must be taken into account when assessing Nasser's professed commitment to the Palestinian struggle, and its implications for Egyptian cinema's representation of the Palestinian issue.[15]

While anti-colonial nationalism had already appeared in Egyptian films of the early 1950s, it was only by the latter half of that decade that a gradual decolonization of the industry began to take place.[16] This turn included the establishment of the Cairo Higher Institute of Cinema in 1959, the first school of its kind in the Arab region, with the aim of training local filmmakers capable of transferring their knowledge to successors.[17] Public-sector involvement was intended to improve filmmaking quality and develop a more politically-engaged cinema than had previously been possible within the capitalist film industry. Egypt's public-sector era did indeed produce higher quality films, not only because of the state subsidy system but also due to the frequent collaborations it facilitated with popular writers of Arabic literature. Tawfik Saleh's *Yawmiyat Na'ib fi al-Aryaf* [*Diary of a Country*

Prosecutor] (1969) is an adaptation of Egyptian author Tawfik al-Hakim's widely-read novel, and his earlier film, *Darb al-Mahabil* [*Alley of Fools*] (1955), while not a product of the public sector, is based on a novel by Egyptian literary giant Naguib Mahfouz, who himself held several important posts —including that of general supervisor —in the Egyptian General Cinema Organization during the 1960s.[18] Yet the industry's nationalization in 1963 did not bring about a radical transformation in the Egyptian mode of cinematic production. Instead it represented a bureaucratic restructuring of the national film sector, with private support still serving a significant economic and ideological function in Egyptian cinematic output.[19]

The introduction of Nasserist economic policy paralleled broad geopolitical shifts set into motion by the Suez Crisis, which had the effect of tipping the regional balance of power in favor of more radically nationalist, internationally non-aligned agendas represented by Egypt and Syria and away from the influence of liberal, Western-dependent regimes such as Jordan, Lebanon and the emergent oil-exporting states of the Arabian peninsula.[20] Yet even though Nasser was vocally committed to Arab socialism and closely aligned with the Socialist Bloc during the Cold War, he never fully conceded to Soviet dictates—or sided with either superpower; rather, his participation in the first Bandung Conference in 1955 crystallized Egypt's preferred approach of "positive neutralism," when a group of Third World countries convened to seek ways of opposing neocolonialism and promoting cultural and economic cooperation.[21] Nonetheless, in an effort to maximize financial and military support for his pan-national project, Nasser continued a post-1952 policy of playing the Cold War superpowers off one another, pragmatically. After the 1952 coup, for instance, when Egypt did not yet have the means by which to embark upon a major military confrontation with Israel, the national leadership accepted aid from the United States, which the latter saw as an investment in Third World anti-communism.[22] Nasser's acceptance of a Czech arms deal in 1955, however, inaugurated a period of rapprochement and profitable relations with the Socialist Bloc that would eventually lead to U.S. disinvestment. The arms deal was offered following a series of aggressive Israeli provocations along the Egyptian border that culminated in the devastating 1955 Gaza Raid (code-named Operation Black Arrow). The material damage and heavy casualties resulting from this confrontation rendered it Egypt's most serious clash with Israel since their signing of an armistice agreement in 1949[23] and persuaded Nasser that Egypt needed to shift emphasis from socioeconomic to military development.[24] The consequences of the Suez Crisis and the Gaza Raid also drastically heightened Egypt's sense of urgency regarding the Palestinian question, justifying a more assertive leadership on the part of Nasser.

As discussed, from the very onset of the 1952 revolution, Egyptian domestic and foreign policy was tied to the loss of Palestine and to Arab aspirations for liberation from imperialism. From the late 1950s and into the 1960s, Egyptian policy toward Palestinian refugees was relatively welcoming, with Nasser inviting Palestinian students to attend Egyptian universities gratis and help staff the nascent public sector. In 1962, Law 66 ensured that Palestinians employed by the Egyptian public sector would be treated "on equal footing with Egyptian nationals."[25] As a result, several key Palestinian cultural workers studied at the Cairo Higher Institute of Cinema and other higher educational institutions in Cairo before going on to contribute to the militant, autonomous Palestinian cinema of the 1970s—whether as filmmakers or in capacities such as union organizers or archivists. Under the post-1948 administration and control of Egypt and Jordan, little possibility existed for Palestinians to establish a cinema industry, which meant that Palestinian filmmakers first worked from sites of exile.[26] Indeed, by the latter half of the 1960s, the paths of budding Palestinian filmmakers Sulafa Jadallah and Ghaleb Chaath as well as of Lebanese-Egyptian filmmaker of Palestine solidarity films, Nabiha Lotfi and Jordanian archivist of revolutionary Palestinian cinema, Khadijah Habashneh, who also worked for the Palestinian women's union, all passed through Cairo. The student and women's unions in which these artists participated were among a total of five Palestinian unions, founded in Cairo, that would become part of the Palestine Liberation Organization (PLO) in 1964.[27] Among the first batches to graduate from the Higher Institute of Cinema in 1964—in fact the first Arab woman ever to study cinematography there—Sulafa Jadallah would go on to become a founding member of the Palestine Film Unit (PFU) in Amman in 1968 alongside Mustafa Abu Ali and Hani Jawhariyyeh.

While hailing from different places and backgrounds, Jadallah, Chaath, Lotfi, and Habashneh were all affiliated with the Palestine liberation movement and part of the same 1960s student generation that would witness the rise and decline of Nasserism and the Arab nationalist left. Egypt and Egyptian cinema offered them a productive site for education, material resources, work opportunities and revolutionary struggle. They also belonged to a generation of Palestine solidarity filmmakers and activists who saw themselves as revolutionary pan-Arabists.[28] Lotfi, after receiving her education at the Cairo Higher Institute of Cinema, became one of the best-known female documentary filmmakers in Egypt and later actively contributed to Palestine revolution cinema.[29] Her younger sister, Arab Loutfi, also trained at the Institute and subsequently created an oeuvre of films that places "the Palestinian issue at the core of regional politics."[30] Chaath exemplifies a Palestinian exiled to Egypt during the Nakba—in his family's case from Jerusalem to Cairo. His trajectory is that of a Palestinian artist-in-exile, an interesting figure who allows us to think not only about how Egyptian cinema represented Palestine on screen, but, in turn, about how Palestinian filmmakers themselves contributed labor and ideas to Egyptian cinema. Chaath traveled to Austria in the early 1960s, where he obtained a diploma in film directing from the Vienna Film Institute in 1967.[31] There he also participated in student organizing and the Palestinian student union[32] before returning to Cairo equipped with a more internationalist outlook and growing revolutionary consciousness regarding the anti-imperialist struggles waged in his two homes, Palestine and Egypt.

The tide of Arab nationalism that initially spearheaded the Palestinian struggle increasingly receded through the course of the 1960s, signaled early on by Syria's secession from the United Arab Republic (UAR) after a mere three years.[33] Syria—which had developed a rendition of Arab nationalism known as Ba'thism—was brought into the Egyptian orbit during the late 1950s, when both states had come to reject alignment with the West while seeking nonetheless to curb communism, and found themselves threatened by incessant Israeli border attacks aimed at undermining both countries' support for the Palestinian resistance.[34] Indeed, the Syrian Ba'thists saw in their union with Egypt a historic opportunity to achieve one of their primary goals: Arab unity.[35] Nasser's domination of the UAR soon fueled factionalism within the union, however, provoking a Syrian military coup in 1961 and consequent secession from the UAR. Israel took advantage of this breakup by creating illegal farming settlements in the Israeli–Syrian demilitarized zone and relentlessly pursuing military and verbal attacks on Syria.[36] The disintegration of the UAR and an ensuing gradual decline of left-leaning Arab nationalism across the region also carried particular implications for the more radical strands of the Palestinian struggle and its networks of support. For instance, by the mid-1960s, Israel had outlawed the Palestinian pan-Arab socialist organization, al-'Ard, founded by Palestinian journalist Fouzi El-Asmar and others who had drawn inspiration from the Nasserist experiment—which paved the way for the founding of the PLO in exile.[37]

Post-Defeat Cinema and the Emergence of the Palestinian Revolutionary Movement

The Naksa represented the culmination of almost two decades of growing tension between Israel and neighboring Arab states, in a third Arab–Israeli war, a further turning point that significantly shaped the course of the Palestinian struggle and Egyptian and Arab politics in general. Following six days of military confrontation—in an exemplary Zionist move, the intention of which was to dominate and control "Greater Israel" (the entire Fertile Crescent, from the Jordan River to the Mediterranean Sea) for ideological-political purposes—Israel managed to gain more of what it regarded as strategic territory: East Jerusalem, the Palestinian West Bank and Gaza Strip, the Syrian Golan Heights / al-Jawlan, and for several years also the Egyptian Sinai Peninsula. The Naksa not only meant military defeat and further territorial losses for the participating Arab armies, but also rendered another approximately 400,000 Palestinians refugees in a second major exodus since the Nakba.[38] According to official Egyptian estimates, approximately 13,000 Palestinian refugees entered Egypt during the course of the Six-Day War and in its immediate wake.[39]

In Egypt, the Defeat exacerbated the grievances of Nasser's critics, whose radicalization had been brewing since the breakdown of the UAR. As such, and in response to increasing discontent with the Arab nationalist regimes, a new Arab left emerged post-1967, one that constituted "a crystallization of the political, ideological, and organizational unrest that the various existing political organizations had been experiencing since the early sixties."[40] Throughout 1968, a series of student and worker-led strikes and protests took place in reaction to the Defeat, to challenge the social compromises and limitations of Nasserism.[41] With respect to Palestine, the events of 1968 were soon to be followed by further student protests in 1971–72, as part of a growing current of political activism that developed after Sadat came to power. This activism was spearheaded by leftist students who had visited Palestinian refugee camps and were inspired by the Palestinian resistance, and who in turn formed the "Society of the Supporters of the Palestinian Revolution."[42] This moment of heightened social tension, dissent and revolutionary ferment among the Arab left, at which the Egyptian state's foreign and domestic policies were vociferously challenged, coincided with the proliferation of a broader left internationalism across the world, a tendency that would reverberate within the cinematic sphere, where transnational collaborations and militant solidarity films were becoming a noticeable new force.

Thus, a period of "self-criticism" after the Defeat ensued among Arab artists and intellectuals, with post-1967 Arab cinema garnering itself the qualification "defeat-conscious" after an influential article on the subject by Tunisian film critic and director, Nouri Bouzid.[43] On the level of content, defeat-conscious films would come to share a commitment to critically examining the Naksa's root causes and sociopolitical consequences. In Egypt, this effort materialized in the form of the New Cinema Group co-founded in Egypt in 1968 by a collective of film and cultural workers including Palestinian filmmaker Ghaleb Chaath and Nabiha Lotfi, who were joined by a group of committed, anti-imperialist cineastes. The collective wrote a manifesto that posed a challenge to the generic conventions and escapist proclivities of commercial melodrama and its complicity with the status quo. The aim of the collective was for cinema to become more political and to focus more on everyday social struggles. The only feature films to come out of the New Cinema Group were Ali Abd El-Khalek's *Ughniyya 'ala al-Mamar* [*A Song on the Passage*] (1972), about five Egyptian soldiers holding their position in a Sinai pass against the Israeli invasion during the 1967 war, and Ghaleb Chaath's *Al-Zilal fi al-Ganib al-Akhar* [*Shadows on the Other Side*] (1973). Paradigmatic of Egypt–Palestine relations during an emerging post-1967 cinema culture, *Shadows on the Other Side* was co-produced by the New Cinema Group and Egypt's already retreating public sector. Dickinson (2018) has therefore appropriately described the film as "something of a half-way house en route to the total privatization of filmmaking."[44] The film was banned in Egypt for a couple of years after the 1973 October War—most likely due to its critical analysis of internal problems that contributed to the Defeat of 1967.[45] Another film that was skeptically received by the Sadat regime is Youssef Chahine's much-acclaimed *Al-'Asfour* [*The Sparrow*] (1972), which is similarly emblematic in its "leftist critique" of the Defeat.[46] In effect, what emerges from a survey and analysis of post-1967 film production, whether in Egypt or across Arab public-sector cinema more generally, is the sense that Palestine and the unresolved Palestinian struggle had become a popular allegorical locus for self-critique and revolutionary aspiration among Arab filmmakers keen to develop a more radical and realist aesthetic. From the late 1960s onward, the Palestinian cause became key to cultivating networks of transnational solidarity and pan-Arab collaboration.[47]

Besides Saleh's *The Dupes*, other Arab films of this period that center paradigmatically on Palestine included *Rijal taht al-Shams* [*Men Under the Sun*] (1970) (not to be confused with the source novella for *The Dupes*) by Marwan Mu'azzin, Muhammad Shahin and Nabil Maleh, Syrian director Khaled Hamada's *Al-Sikkin* (1972), *Kafr Kassem* (1974) by the Lebanese Borhane Alaouié (but also supported by the Syrian NFO), and the documentary films of the Iraqi al-Zubaidi. Of noteworthy influence on these Arab film productions were the documentaries made by the Palestinian Film Unit, which documented relevant events and Palestinian living conditions with an ideologically militant bent. According to Palestinian-Syrian film critic Bashar Ibrahim, these films made a strong impression on Tawfik Saleh, Mohammad Malas and many other Arab filmmakers of the period.[48] These region-wide efforts to create new and more political forms of cinema paralleled the emergence of the Palestinian-led armed guerilla struggle, just as the latter would inspire the formation of a first autonomous Palestine Film Unit that would document and produce militant films about the struggle.[49] The Israeli seizure and occupation of additional Palestinian territory in 1967, and the discrediting effect the Naksa had on pan-Arab nationalism had catalyzed the seeds of the Palestinian revolutionary movement which had already begun to consolidate during the lead-up to the war.

In fact, the national revolutionary movement in Palestine had a long history of engaging in armed struggle for the purposes of achieving political end. As early as the British Mandate, Palestinians used armed struggle against the British imperialists as well as the encroaching Zionist settlers.[50] Until the Naksa, which bolstered Palestinian nationalism as a political call, Palestinian political activity had largely come under the patronage of the respective Palestinian leaderships in exile. In an effort to highlight his commitment to Palestine, Nasser played an instrumental role in the foundation of the PLO under the auspices of the Cairo-based Arab League. The motivation for creating the organization was ostensibly to assist Palestinians in achieving at least a modicum of self-determination, yet the PLO was neither entirely autonomous nor "truly representative of the Palestinian people."[51] The PLO eventually went on to marginalize its more radical, left-wing sub-groupings which, in the wake of the Six-Day War, would practice a more militant program than that of the organization's bourgeois-leaning founders.[52] Indeed, 1967 shifted the balance of power to the Palestinian guerilla fighters (*fedayeen*) and away from the "elitist establishment of the PLO, which the Palestinians associated with the defeated Arab states."[53] Promoting armed struggle as a more effective method of political action for confronting Zionism, several exclusively Palestinian organizations, which had already started to form underground, came to the fore. As such, the various small guerilla groups that had already been involved in activities independent of the PLO prior to the Naksa proliferated.[54] Fatah, covertly formed by a group of Palestinians including Yasser Arafat in Kuwait in 1959, would become the most important of these.[55] Increasingly skeptical of Nasser's pan-Arab promises and policies with respect to the struggle for Palestinian liberation, and increasingly aware of the successes of guerilla warfare further afield, Fatah's aim was for Palestine to be "liberated by the Palestinians themselves through armed struggle."[56] Interestingly, Fatah's nascent tactics and rhetoric would mirror the earliest stages of autonomous Palestinian revolutionary filmmaking with respect to its political and cinematic form. As Nick Denes (2014) has generatively put it, the Palestine Film Unit "pursued a cinema synchronized to the revolution's exploratory pulse."[57] In other words, cinematic form was developing in tandem with the revolution—through struggle. This revolutionary Palestinian cinematic form was arguably partly rooted in the late 1960s Egyptian radical cinema discussed above, before it was put into practice in Jordan and Lebanon throughout the decade that followed.

Attending to the Palestinian Perspective: Toward a Situated Representation of Palestine

The Dupes (1972) adapts Ghassan Kanafani's novella *Men in the Sun* to cinematically narrate the collective struggle of three exiled Palestinian "men in the sun." As mentioned, adaptations of Arabic literary works to cinema was common practice in the history of national Arab cinemas,[58] and represented instances of collaboration amongst Arab artists, notably during this period of discontent with the political status quo and heightened calls for solidarity with Palestine—*The Dupes* being a case in point. Kanafani himself was a Palestinian refugee, meaning that his detailed and realistic descriptions of the Palestinian struggle effectively served as testimonial material.[59]

In the film, Abu Qais (Mohamed Kheir-Halouani), Assad (Bassan Lofti Abou-Ghazala), and Marwan (Saleh Kholoki), whose fragmented histories and memories of Palestine are introduced and interwoven as flashbacks in the first third of the narrative, are brought together in the Shatt el-Arab river location of Basra, an important transit point in Iraq for migrants attempting to access Kuwait. There the three men are joined by a fourth protagonist, Abu Khayzuran (Abderrahman Alrahy), aspects of whose own traumatic memories are similarly related during the second half of the film. These flashbacks are triggered by visual connotations such as shots of the sun, or by verbal reminders in the dialogue, where keywords like "road" or "marriage" evoke unpleasant memories of flight and family problems which are then projected onscreen as brief re-enactments of past events. Corresponding structurally to the first three chapters of the novella—respectively, "Abu Qais," "Assad," and "Marwan"—the first three flashback sequences serve to contextualize how and why the Palestinian men have come to Basra: in essence, they each hail from a different generation and exilic location, representing a cross-section of Palestinian society; and while each one remembers Palestine and the Nakba in a personal way, they evidently share a strong attachment to the homeland. The men all hope to make their way clandestinely through the desert and across the Iraqi border to Kuwait in order to find work for the purpose of supporting their families left behind—the Gulf clearly luring with its oil capital. The expository flashbacks furthermore function as brief but necessary narrative detours that articulate a sense of synchronicity across the men's predicaments, before the rest of the narrative turns more linear and deterministic.

Over the course of the narrative, the film creates a progressive overlap of differing character perspectives and between past and present. While the introductory flashbacks occur more or less consecutively, their first viewing may cause confusion, as past and present veritably blend into one another, and it is not always clear whose perspective is being dramatized. This aesthetic tactic of disorientation, besides conveying a realistic sense of historical displacement, also hinders the spectator from identifying with an overarching hero. Unlike the early 1950s melodramas, in which an Egyptian protagonist's trajectory drives forward the linear narrative while Palestinian characters are explicitly differentiated, the multi-perspectival, polyphonic and temporality-switching style of *The Dupes* is a common feature of post-1967 Arab cinema.[60] Egyptian cinema has in fact produced a number of exemplary multi-perspectival films, such as the previously mentioned public-sector/New Cinema Group co-production, *Shadows on the Other Side* (1973). This film revolves around four students, three of them Egyptian and one Palestinian, enrolled at the College of Art in Cairo, whose divergent and at times clashing personalities are juxtaposed in order to render an ideologically more complex critique of the late 1960s situation—in line with the intellectual tendency of "self-criticism after the Defeat."[61]

In *The Dupes*, the separate but converging narrative strands illustrate not only a set of intersecting Palestinian experiences and perspectives but also hint, progressively, at the problems of factionalism and of the challenging task of organizing a unified political struggle. Representative of the pre-Nakba generation of Palestinians, Abu Qais' exilic narrative strand sets the tone of the film, with the camera facing a vast desert scape, the horizon splitting the frame into sky and land. This first shot places the spectator into a narrative space that is neither temporally nor spatially delineated, evoking cinematically a sense of displacement. When a small, barely visible figure emerges on the horizon, the camera moves to approach what we come to recognize as the visibly lost and stumbling man, Abu Qais. These shots, mostly long-shots, are interspersed with occasional shots of the sun, a poetic motif throughout the narrative—less a temporal marker than a constant reminder of the glaring reality of exile. In contrast to this first scene of encounter, a slow zoom-out will be deployed repeatedly later in the film to reframe the truck carrying the three Palestinians apparently disappearing into the seemingly infinite desert space. These perspectival shifts foreground, on the one hand, the centrality of Palestinian perspectives and, on the other, critique their collective invisibility within the broader, deserted landscape—a metaphor for the geopolitical map at that time.

Once Qais' figure finally reaches the center of the frame, a cut to his point-of-view shifts our focus to a fertile strip along the desolate horizon. Zooming in, the camera lens enacts the elderly man's dream-like approach to what initially appears like an oasis but turns out to be Basra. The camera then comes to a stop as Abu Qais is portrayed halting at the roots of a tree, against which he rests his visibly

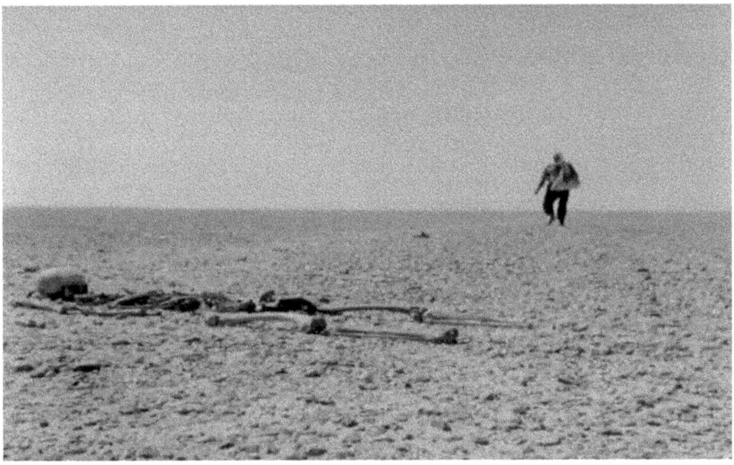

Figure 2.1 *The Dupes* [*Al-Makhdu'un*] (Tawfik Saleh, Syria, 1972).

exhausted body. The melancholic, non-diegetic flute music previously introduced now fades out, transitioning into diegetic bird sounds that create a peaceful and natural atmosphere along with a sense of lived time. The camera subsequently shows Abu Qais lying on the ground head-on, while running his hands through the soil, rendering an intimate, haptic connection between body and land. As he talks about how the scent of the earth reminds him of his wife's wet hair, Qais' voice-over joins the sound of chirping birds, creating an audiovisual interplay that evokes his affective relationship to the land, associated as it is with memories of his wife in Palestine and a life before the Nakba.

Flashbacks to Qais' village life, triggered as he gazes at the Shatt el-Arab from his seated position under the tree, convey the idea that Qais, a peasant, is deeply attached to his home/land. Multiple close-ups of cacti and olive groves and, then again, of his face, invoke memories of a Palestinian past that precedes not only Zionist settler-colonialism and eventual secular pan-Arabism but also the ruptures caused by modernization more generally, lending the film an anti-imperialist tone. The Shatt al-Arab in this context comes furthermore to represent a visual site of reflection for Qais that is enhanced by the wailing vocal sounds of *mawwal*, a traditional genre of vocal music represented and popularized in many Egyptian films.[62] The Shatt al-Arab scene also prompts a connection between the film and its pan-Arab context, in that it denotes both Qais' exilic location, away from Palestine, and evokes, through the resounding voice-over of his childhood teacher Ustaz Selim, a geographical space from "the Nile to the Euphrates"—recalling the kind of rhetoric Nasser famously propagated to the Persian/Arabian Gulf in his famous Sawt al-Arab radio show. The reflexivity of these juxtapositions between past and present is underscored by a series of idyllic village life scenes interspersed with archival, photographic footage depicting various political agreements and events pertaining to the Nakba (including images of barbed wires and food distribution queues in refugee camps) that serve to highlight its disruptive effect on Palestinian lives.

Qais' exilic character position and narrative arc may also suggest an analogy to director Saleh's personal trajectory as a migrating artist and to other solidarity filmmakers (in)directly associated with Palestine (such as Chaath and al-Zubaidi). Saleh was but one Arab artist compelled to cross borders, in his case from Egypt to Syria, due to restrictions at home. He was an ardent critic of bourgeois nationalism's exclusionary nature, and his most renowned film would seem to link the limits he experienced of statist pan-Arabism to the unleashing of a far more radical pan-Arabism. The Dupes invites us to consider the interdependence of apparently disparate social struggles for liberation as well as the significance of the Palestinian struggle to the revolutionary aspirations of Saleh and his artistic Arab contemporaries.

Complex Temporality and Borders as Allegory of Palestinian Reality

The encounter of the three Palestinian men in Basra, a liminal site of arrival and departure, figures as a significant narrative turning point in *The Dupes*. Situated within a complex narrative-compositional structure that, by intricately interweaving the various backstories through flashbacks, confers agency upon Palestinian subjectivity, this encounter avers an urgent need for a unified solution to the Palestinian question and a fundamental transformation of Palestinian reality. Complex temporality is in this context a central characteristic of a Palestinian reality for which ongoing struggle is contingent upon a hopeful future as well as shared memories of a Palestinian past.

It is in Basra, away from their homeland in Palestine, that the men are talked into a collective deal with self-appointed smuggler, Abu Khayzuran, who offers to drive them across the desert in his truck at a bargain rate. Since Khayzuran regularly delivers goods to a Kuwaiti merchant, he claims that his truck is less likely to arouse suspicion at the border. Yet the three men soon learn that the endeavor is far from risk-free, for they are told they will be obliged to hide inside the truck's stifling empty water tank in the middle of the hot desert while their driver clears border controls both leaving Iraq and entering Kuwait. That way, the truck can appear to pass for its intended purpose, that of transporting goods. Before the men hesitantly agree to board the big black truck, the camera sweeps around the vehicle, as if it were a special exhibit in a museum, with ominous music by the Syrian composer Solhi al-Wadi underscoring the dramatic effect. In this way, an impending crisis is already sketched out through subtle foreshadowing techniques. When Khayzuran asks whether the men have made their decision to board his truck, the camera follows them as they walk toward the back of the tank in which they would be required to wait, while a hollow banging noise becomes audible on the soundtrack. This banging will in fact be repeated, diegetically, during the film's much later, fateful knocking scene, when it will be heard emanating from within the tank in which the helpless migrants are stuck. In effect, the Basra scenes serve to predict a bleak future for the protagonists—not least by depicting acts of negotiation and agreements that are all too familiar in the history of the Palestinian struggle and in which the very Palestinians who stand to benefit most from them have had little or no say.

At the same time, the geographical crossroads of Basra represent a momentary semblance of opportunity for the three migrants, who have traveled to this place out of genuine hope, notwithstanding their journey's fatal outcome. Remaining true to the novella, the film is set in 1958, during the peak period of pan-Arab nationalism and during the very year in which the formation of the United Arab Republic put Nasser's vision of Arab unity into political practice. As noted earlier, this was also the time when the Palestinian resistance was still largely under the helm of the respective Arab states hosting Palestinians in exile. The film was made more than a decade after those events, however, by which point the PLO was already an established organization, and autonomous militant alternatives were

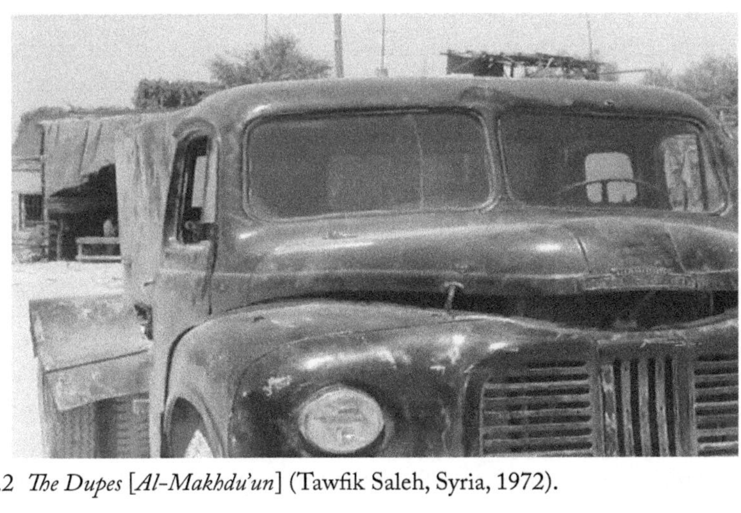

Figure 2.2 *The Dupes* [*Al-Makhdu'un*] (Tawfik Saleh, Syria, 1972).

already beginning to be organized. This difference in time facilitates an allegorical reading of Abu Khayzuran as a signifier for a corrupt Palestinian leader (Arafat) or even a Nasserist one.[63] Scholarly interpretations of the novella frequently make this analogy, suggesting that the smugglers depicted in Basra evoke the political corruption associated with the contemporary Arab leaders and their regimes.[64] Yet Saleh himself ostensibly contested this interpretation, stating that for him, Abu Khayzuran, who promises to drive the three Palestinian migrants from Basra to Kuwait only to become partly responsible for their collective death at the end of the film, does not represent Arab governments so much as the direction of the Palestinian resistance before 1967.[65]

The three men agree to Abu Khayzuran's offer after their respective narrative strands converge, whereupon the potentiality of a collective struggle as a premise for change is set into motion. A particularly striking way in which the film illustrates this shift from individual to collective outlook is its manner of lending precedence to individual lenses during the first half of the film, then switching to potentially shared lenses afterwards. During the travel sequence, the front window of the truck figures as one such shared lens—a screen onto the future—but one which is not ultimately accessible to all of the travelers. The film's second half thus formally pursues a common journey within a temporality that unfolds on the run. In this sense, the truck becomes a microcosm of both the external and internal constraints facing Palestinians in their contemporary reality. Just as it contains, under one roof, characters who represent differing strands of Palestinian society and its struggle for liberation, the truck is finally controlled by Abu Khayzuran, repeated insert shots of whose wristwatch made visible near the steering wheel indicate his responsibility for determining the speed and direction of (the) Palestinian movement. By devoting extended screen time to this precarious situation in advance of any tangible destination, the film suggests a critique of the status quo and its failure to hold out a just solution for the Palestinians, instead foregrounding its continual postponement and displacement.

Besides the fragmented memories of Palestine established through flashbacks at the beginning of *The Dupes* that, together, construct a veritable collective Palestinian consciousness, the three men are also characterized as sharing the experience of being exploited at national borders and by representatives of state authority. Not only do borders figure as a strategy for narrative tension in *The Dupes*, they arguably allegorize—especially in juxtaposition with the desert space—the limitations and contradictions of regional geopolitics concerning the Palestinian issue. The critical depiction of these sites gestures to the legacy of colonialism and to neocolonial power dynamics under the neoliberalism that was emerging across the region from the early 1970s. As the narrative proceeds, it becomes clear that Abu Khayzuran is just as prone to corruption, and drawn to profit, as the border authorities depicted in the film. During the border scenes at which he places the lives of his Palestinian passengers in jeopardy, the narrative temporality is suspensefully foregrounded; power unfolds as the domain of those in control of time at the expense of the Palestinians for whom time is running out. These border scenes thus mark the ability of the omnipresent, all-powerful state to control Palestinian destiny. Their critical depiction underlines the film's critique of an abiding system of postcolonial Arab nation-states for which the struggle for Palestinian liberation has been subordinated to national interests rationalized through subsumption under the pan-Arab umbrella. The tense border encounters in *The Dupes* repeatedly expose the obstacles to Palestinian self-determination by illustrating how Palestinians are perpetually abandoned by all authorities and potential allies along the way.

After Basra, where temporality expands to account for the time of waiting and negotiation, timelessness predominates in the desert. The barely moving camera in these scenes suggests stasis and geographical ambiguity; it is only the truck's movement that provides a sense of progression through time and space. Throughout the journey, the truck is shown occasionally in close-up and at other times from afar, situating the spectator into multiple ranges and perspectives vis-à-vis the Palestinians consistently captured by the camera's gaze. Thus, self-reflexive techniques aver to Palestinian visibility, just as the isolated truck embodies a state of containment and exclusion and, as a vehicle being used for the illicit transport of migrant labor, draws attention to the lure of Gulf capital for Arab workers across the region. These cynical conditions notwithstanding, *The Dupes* does not

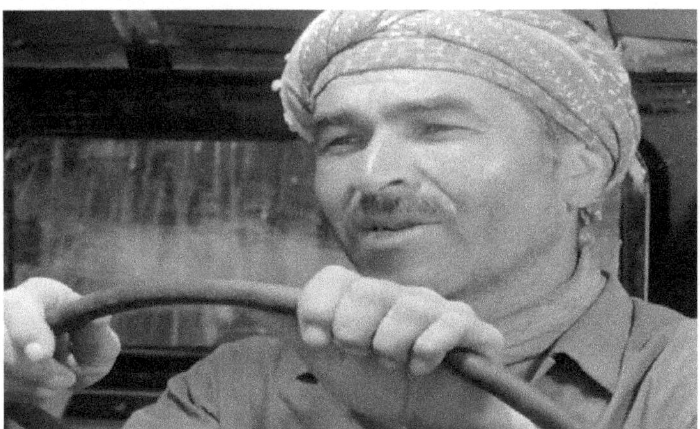

Figure 2.3 *The Dupes* [*Al-Makhdu'un*] (Tawfik Saleh, Syria, 1972).

portray Palestinians as passive victims of their circumstances. Rather, the film as a whole cinematically enacts their struggle and foregrounds their perspectives, demonstrably returning to them their agency by the penultimate scene. In this way, *The Dupes* performs aesthetically the historical turn toward an independent revolutionary Palestinian movement following the Naksa through a subtle yet strikingly effective concluding plot twist.

The Function of Sound as Political Resistance

In Egypt and in Palestine, the decade following *Men in the Sun*'s publication was an eventful period, punctuated by the 1967 Defeat. The Six-Day War, which not only exacerbated the Palestinian issue but also negatively affected pan-Arab efforts to achieve regional unity, inspired Tawfik Saleh to make a conscious, if minor plot change to Kanafani's novella—in effect, to create a "politicized adaptation" of the earlier, literary work.[66] Already a forerunner of early neorealist filmmaking in Egypt from the mid-1950s, when adaptations such as *Al-Bab al-Maftouh* [*The Open Door*] (1963) by Henry Barakat were evidencing a more politicized Egyptian cinema, Saleh was radicalized by the period's significant turn of historical events, becoming more aware of their implications for the Palestinian resistance movement that emerged after the novella's publication.

As the filmic narrative shifts from the more hopeful scenes of encounter and departure in Basra to the actual road trip through the desert en route to Kuwait, events take a turn for the worse. The scene at issue occurs toward the end of the film, once the truck reaches the second border control, the entry to Kuwaiti territory which emerges seemingly out of nowhere in the vast desert. As Abu Khayzuran presses his foot solidly on the breaks, a suspended temporality characteristic of the previous border scenes is re-introduced. Abu Khayzuran hurriedly exits the truck and enters an office where two inspectors are waiting, while the three Palestinian migrants are made to await their driver's return inside the stifling water tank. Although their suffering is never shown explicitly, the film heightens spectatorial suspense through editing techniques that produce the sense of a torturously long wait during which the spectator may project onto the (non-)action memories of an early border scene in which the migrants, who survive a first long wait in the truck, emerge from it covered in perspiration and physically spent. As the driver responsible for relieving his passengers from their unbearable confinement rushes to complete a document inspection process, the camera alternates between the interior and exterior of the border office, rendering urgency and an intensifying sense of lost Palestinian time. Indeed, as the camera cuts to inside the office, where an artificially prolonged dialogue between Abu Khayzuran and two Kuwaiti inspectors does not seem as though it will ever conclude, despite the former's increasingly desperate efforts, a series of surveillance-like shots from inside out, placing the truck at a visual distance, remind us of the powerful actors who are really in control of Palestinian fate.

It is ultimately through an urgent banging noise—interrupted intermittently by brief cuts to the office interior, and reminiscent of the earlier scene in Basra—that the entrapped Palestinians are rendered audible, trapped inside the tank. The scene thus alternates between quick takes of the truck and longer takes of Abu Khayzuran occupied by the inspectors inside. Thus, creating a Brechtian distanciation device by which the spectator is at once situated and unsettled in her position as passive onlooker, Saleh renders the scene a general appeal by Palestinians to the outside listener, a shout-out against the oppressive effects of nationalism / national borders on the Palestinian cause. After the Kuwaitis finally sign Khayzuran's papers, and the truck speeds off to a safe distance where he can allow the men out, he makes a fatal discovery: upon opening the tank he finds the three men have suffocated to death. In a bleak concluding scene, he disposes of their bodies before driving off—a final act of abandonment before the credits roll.

This ending is quite different from that of Kanafani's original novella, in which the three entrapped Palestinians remain silent (or are unheard?), in effect obeying Abu Khayzuran's request to wait patiently in the stifling tank. Saleh's cinematic rendition of the story thus transforms the Palestinians' confinement into an audible and therefore more overt act of resistance, demonstrating how a situation of opportunism, wherein Palestinian resistance could only be postulated, may become a real opportunity for change. The conscious insertion of the sound of the Palestinians desperately knocking from inside the tank was a decidedly political move which enabled the filmic narrative to end on a very different note, one of urgent challenge regarding the accelerating contemporary turn within the Palestinian movement toward collective armed resistance.

The Dupes is not the only Egyptian/Arab film produced in the post-1967 period to thematize the Palestine turn to armed resistance,[67] although it certainly serves as a paradigmatic example. As Yaqub (2011) concisely puts it, "*The Dupes* was not only part of a new post-1967 Palestinian consciousness but a milestone in the development of a new Arab cinema and the byproduct of the complex relationship between Arab politics and the Palestine question."[68] For Saleh, making such a film required working abroad. The social realist cinema which he and his contemporaries were practically theorizing focused on marginalized subjects and pressing political issues and, in the process, connected social struggles, including the Palestinian liberation movement, to each another. With this in mind, it is possible to articulate the allegory of *The Dupes* to Egyptian revolutionary aspirations at the time. *The Dupes* analyzes contradictions within the Palestinian struggle and the pan-Arab political landscape at large, while implicitly calling for a more radical pan-Arabism. It exposes the challenges of reconciling the motives of individual Palestinians, who go to Kuwait in search of economic reward, with the collective struggle for liberation from those very motives and weighs the risks of dependence upon corrupt compatriots and authority figures. In the context of the next chapter, jumping three decades forward, the lure and growing dominance of Gulf capital symbolically referenced in *The Dupes* have become an undeniable reality for Arab states into the new millennium,[69] rendering the geopolitical conditions for Palestinian liberation increasingly dire, while effectively creating a broader and much more global Palestinian resistance.

Notes

1 The element of trade relations would become a cornerstone of the normalization process, from 1979 onward. See Ann Lesch and Mark A. Tessler, *Israel, Egypt, and the Palestinians: From Camp David to Intifada* (Indianapolis: Indiana University Press, 1989), 68–72.

2 See Rasha Salti, "Critical Nationals: The Paradoxes of Syrian Cinema," in *Insights into Syrian Cinema: Essays and Conversations with Contemporary Filmmakers*, ed. Rasha Salti (New York: Rattapallax, 2006), 26.

3 Tamara Maatouk clarifies that the so-called Cinema Support Institution (CSI) had already emerged in 1957, whereas the General Egyptian Institution for Cinema, Radio, and Television was established in 1963: "Th[e] private character of the film industry began to falter when the Egyptian government established the Cinema Support Institution (Mu'assassat da'm al-sinima) on 2 June 1957, officially marking the birth of the public sector in Egyptian cinema" (Maatouk, "Understanding the Public Sector in Egyptian Cinema: A State Venture," *Cairo Papers in Social Science* 35, no. 3 (2019): 7; see also 14–19, 33–7).

4 For instance, Youssef Chahine's *Al-'Asfour* [*The Sparrow*] (1972) was co-funded by Algeria's Office national pour le commerce et l'industrie cinématographique (ONCIC), Salah Abu Seif went to Iraq and Tawfik Saleh to Syria to make *The Dupes*.

5 For overview, see "Syria" entry in Terri Ginsberg and Chris Lippard, *Historical Dictionary of Middle Eastern Cinema* (Lanham, MD: The Scarecrow Press, 2020), 459–60. See also Kay Dickinson, *Arab Cinema Travels: Transnational Syria, Palestine, Dubai and Beyond* (London: British Film Institute, 2016).

6 Kay Dickinson, "The State of Labor and Labor for the State: Syrian and Egyptian Cinema beyond the 2011 Uprisings," Framework: The Journal of Cinema and Media 53, no. 1 (2012): 102.

7 Salti, "Critical Nationals," 26. See also Nadia Yaqub, *Palestinian Cinema in the Days of Revolution* (Austin: University of Texas Press, 2018), 90–4.

8 Dickinson, *Arab Cinema Travels*, 49.

9 Dickinson, "The State of Labor," 106.

10 Livia Alexander, foreword to Salti, *Insights into Syrian Cinema*, 13.

11 Tareq Y. Ismael, *The Arab Left* (Syracuse, NY: Syracuse University Press, 1976), 80.

12 Mahmoud Hussein, *Class Conflict in Egypt: 1945–1970* (New York and London: Monthly Review Press, 1973).

13 See Anouar Abdel-Malek, "Nasserism And Socialism," *Socialist Register* 1 (March 1964): 38–55; and Adam Hanieh, *Lineages of Revolt: Issues of Contemporary Capitalism in the Middle East* (Chicago: Haymarket, 2013), 25–26.

14 "Nasser's decision to imprison large numbers of Muslim Brotherhood members, as well as inflict severe torture on many of them, meant the decimation of the Brotherhood for most of the 1950s and 1960s" (Sara Salem, *Anticolonial Afterlives in Egypt: The Politics of Hegemony* (Cambridge, UK: Cambridge University Press, 2020), 113).

15 Ismael, *The Arab Left*, 18–19.

16 Sabrina Joseph, "Representations of Private/Public Domains: The Feminine Ideal and Modernist Agendas in Egyptian Film, Mid–1950s–1980s," *Frontiers: A Journal of Women Studies* 30, no. 2 (2009): 75.

17 Malek Khouri, *The Arab National Project in Youssef Chahine's Cinema* (Cairo: American University in Cairo Press, 2010), 54.

18 Samia Mehrez, *Egyptian Writers Between History and Fiction: Essays on Naguib Mahfouz, Sonallah Ibrahim, and Gamal Al-Ghitani* (Cairo: American University in Cairo Press, 1994), 149.

19 Qussai Samak, "The Politics of Egyptian Cinema," *MERIP Reports*, no. 56 (April 1977): 13. See also Tamara Maatouk, who discusses how "the film private sector, [which] continued to own the majority of cinematic resources." ("Understanding the Public Sector," 27.)

20 Samih K. Farsoun and Christina Zacharia Hawatmeh, *Palestine and the Palestinians* (Boulder, CO: Westview Press, 1997), 175.

21 Ismael, *The Arab Left*, 81.

22 Ray Takeyh notes that "American policy toward the Middle East must be viewed in the context of Cold War rivalry, in which the Eisenhower administration sought to incorporate the Arab world in its global alliance network. In pursuit of this aim, the American policymakers recognized the potency of regional nationalism and the importance of Egypt in determining the direction of Arab politics. Accordingly, the Eisenhower administration sought to guide the Egyptian regime along lines conducive to its Cold War objectives" (Takeyh, *The Origins of the Eisenhower Doctrine: The US, Britain and Nasser's Egypt, 1953–57* (London: Palgrave Macmillan, 2000), ix).

23 Avi Shlaim, *The Iron Wall: Israel and the Arab World* (New York: W.W. Norton, 2001), 124.

24 Shlaim, *The Iron Wall*, 126.

25 Oroub El-Abed, *Unprotected: Palestinians in Egypt since 1948* (Washington, ON: Institute for Palestine Studies / International Development Research Centre, 2009), xviii.

26 Kay Dickinson, *Arab Film and Video Manifestos: Forty-Five Years of the Moving Image Amid Revolution* (Cham, Switzerland: Palgrave Macmillan, 2018), 82. See also Viviane Saglier, "'Not-Yet' an Industry: The Temporalities of Contemporary Palestinian Cinema," in *Cinema of the Arab World: Contemporary Directions in Theory and Practice*, eds. Terri Ginsberg and Chris Lippard (Cham, Switzerland: Palgrave Macmillan, 2020), 125–46.

27 El-Abed, *Unprotected*, xix.

28 Terri Ginsberg, *Films of Arab Loutfi and Heiny Srour: Studies in Palestine Solidarity Cinema* (Cham, Switzerland: Palgrave Macmillan, 2021), 52.

29 Nabiha Lotfy made several experimental documentary films, such as the PLO production *Li'anna al-Judhur La Tamut* [*Because Roots Don't Die*] (1977), about women and their memories of the Tel al-Za'tar camp massacre that took place during the Lebanese Civil War in 1976. She also co-founded the New Cinema Group with the Palestinian filmmaker, Ghaleb Chaath. For more about Nabiha Lotfy, see Yaqub, *Palestinian Cinema*, 55, 165–6.

30 See Ginsberg, *Films of Arab Loutfi and Heiny Srour*, 4.

31 Khadijah Habashneh, *Fursan Al-Sinima: Sira Wahdat Aflam Filastin* (Amman: Al-Ahlia lil-Nashr wal-Tawzi', 2019), 113, 128. Chaath went on to make films within the PLO in Beirut by the mid-1970s, by which point other Palestinian organizations, such as the Popular Front for the Liberation of Palestine (PFLP), the Popular Democratic Front for the Liberation of Palestine (PDFLP) and the PLO's arts and culture section, had begun to engage in film production. He also founded Samed, a film production unit that would belong to Fatah. Two films came out of this period: *Al-Miftah* [*The Key*] (1976) and *Yawm al-Ard* [*Land Day*] (1978). See Yaqub, *Palestinian Cinema*, 148; and Dickinson, *Arab Film and Video Manifestos*, 90.

32 For more on Palestine solidarity and student politics, see Sorcha Thomson, Pelle Valentin Olsen, and Sune Haugbolle, "Palestine Solidarity Conferences in the Global Sixties," *Journal of Palestine Studies* 51, no. 1 (January 2022): 27–49.

33 Ismael, *The Arab Left*, 92–3.

34 Joel Beinin, "The Communist Movement and Nationalist Political Discourse in Nasirist Egypt," *Middle East Journal* 41, no. 4 (1987): 580. A key reason for Nasser's crackdown on communists was to counteract developments in neighboring Iraq, where the revolutionary Qasim regime, which had overthrown the Iraqi monarchy in 1958, was building a strategic alliance with the Iraqi Communist Party (ICP), posing a powerful threat to Egypt's regional ambitions.

35 Ismael, *The Arab Left*, 25.

36 Ghada Karmi, *Married to Another Man: Israel's Dilemma in Palestine* (London: Pluto Press, 2015), 25.

37 Fouzi El-Asmar, "Continuing the Palestinian Struggle, Part 2," interview by Terri Ginsberg, *ZNet* 8 October 2021, https://www.academia.edu/2029583/Continuing_the_Palestinian_Struggle_Part_2. The first resurgence of Palestinian nationalism since the 1948 Nakba, Al-Ard had formed in 1959 out of a failed attempt to bring together Arab nationalists and communists in the Arab Front and would soon develop links, albeit short-lived, with the PLO. For more, see Yezid Sayigh, *Armed Struggle and the Search for State: The Palestinian National Movement, 1949–1993* (Oxford and New York: Oxford University Press, 1997), 38.

38 Farsoun and Hawatmeh, *Palestine*, 138.

39 El-Abed, *Unprotected*, 28.

40 Ismael, *The Arab Left*, 101.

41 Ahmed Abdallah, *The Student Movement and National Politics in Egypt, 1923–1973* (London: Al Saqi, 1985), 140, 149–75.

42 Abdallah, *The Student Movement*, 176–77.

43 Nouri Bouzid, "New Realism in Arab Cinema: The Defeat-Conscious Cinema," *Alif: Journal of Comparative Poetics*, 15 (1995): 242–50.

44 Kay Dickinson, *Arab Film and Video Manifestos*, 45.

45 Viola Shafik, "Cinema in Palestine," in *Companion Encyclopedia of Middle Eastern and North African Film*, ed. Oliver Leaman (London; New York: Routledge, 2001), 520.

46 Dickinson, *Arab Film and Video Manifestos*, 38.

47 Yaqub, *Palestinian Cinema*, 89.
48 Samirah Alkassim and Nezar Andary, *The Cinema of Muhammad Malas* (Cham, Switzerland: Palgrave Macmillan, 2018), 53.
49 Dickinson, *Arab Film and Video Manifestos*, 81–106.
50 Sameer Abraham, "The PLO at the Crossroads: Moderation, Encirclement, Future Prospects," *MERIP Reports*, no. 80 (1979): 5–26.
51 El-Abed, *Unprotected*, 127.
52 For example, the Marxist-Leninist PFLP (founded by George Habash in 1967—a leading member of which was in fact Ghassan Kanafani). For more on these leftist factions, see Yezid Sayigh, "Armed Struggle and State Formation," *Journal of Palestine Studies* 26, no. 4 (1997): 17–32. See also Sayigh, *Armed Struggle and the Search for State: The Palestinian National Movement, 1949–1993* (Oxford and New York: Oxford University Press, 1997).
53 Farsoun and Hawatmeh, *Palestine*, 181.
54 Sayigh, "Armed Struggle," 19–20.
55 Ismael, *The Arab Left*, 94.
56 Yaqub, *Palestinian Cinema*, 5.
57 Denes, Nick. "Between Form and Function," *Middle East Journal of Culture and Communication* 7, no. 2 (2014): 220, 226.
58 Producing cinematic realism in particular was encouraged by way of collaboration between writers and filmmakers, which led to "a boom in literary adaptations" (Viola Shafik, *Arab Cinema* (Cairo: American University in Cairo Press, 2007), 122).
59 Kanafani's biography somewhat mirrors the trajectories of the characters in his novel: He too was expelled from Acca during the Nakba and was exiled in various Arab states, including Kuwait and Lebanon, where he later settled. In Beirut, he would become an active member of the PFLP alongside George Habash and shared the latter's view that the solution to the Palestinian issue could not be achieved without a social revolution throughout the Arab world. Kanafani was killed in 1972—the year of *The Dupes'* release—in a car bomb explosion for which the Israeli Mossad claimed responsibility. Recognized as a prominent intellectual and writer, Kanafani has since received critical acclaim for his literary output, with *Men in the Sun* perhaps his greatest success. See Barbara Harlow, "History and Endings: Ghassan Kanafani's Men in the Sun and Tawfiq Salih's *The Duped*," *Minnesota Review* 25, no. 1 (1985): 108.
60 Khouri similarly describes Chahine's *The Sparrow* as "polyphonic" with a "multiplicity of characters as they relate and interact with economic corruption, as it, in turn, interacts with the political events that are unfolding on the front with Israel" (Khouri, *The Arab National Project*, 99).
61 *Self-Criticism after the Defeat* (1968; London: Saqi, 2012), by Syrian philosopher Sadik al-Azm, was an influential text to emerge out of the 1967 crisis. It exposes "the political and cultural faults that led to the defeat."
62 Walter Armbrust, "Audiovisual Media and History of the Arab Middle East," in *Middle East Historiographies: Narrating the Twentieth Century*, eds. I. Gershoni, Amy Singer, and Y. Hakan Erdem (Seattle: University of Washington Press, 2006), 301.
63 In an interview, Palestinian revolutionary filmmaker Mostafa Abou Ali commented on this analogy, stating that there are without a doubt certain elements—both in the novella and film—that seem to indicate that Nasser himself was being put into question by Kanafani (my translation). (Guy Hennebelle and Khayati Khemaïs, *La Palestine et le cinéma* (Paris: Éditions du Centenaire), 1977), 41.

64 Harlow, "History," 104.

65 Hennebelle and Khemaïs, *La Palestine et le cinéma*, 41.

66 Harlow, "History," 107.

67 For instance, Palestinian director Ghaleb Chaath's *Shadows on the Other Side*, which was co-produced by the Egyptian public sector, depicts a similar shift. In the course of the narrative, as the student protagonists develop their respective graduation projects at the Fine Arts College in Cairo, Palestinian student Omar's project changes in a meaningful way that corresponds to the historical moment: the emergence of militant armed Palestinian struggle. Although he had initially dedicated himself to a photography project on the issue of Palestinian refugees, he comes up with a different plan once he hears and learns about the Palestinian resistance forming in the Jordan Valley: "I think I want to do something about the *muqawamah*" (resistance). By way of shifting Palestinian images such as this one, the film also raises questions about the appropriate representation of Palestinians in the late 1960s context, advocating for a move away from the documentation of refugee misery to the foregrounding, instead, of *fedayeen* engaged in armed struggle.

68 Yaqub, "The Dupes," 118.

69 From the early 1970s, "virtually all Arab states were laying the groundwork for strict neoliberal economic programs that would be launched under the auspices of the IMF and World Bank" (Hanieh, *Lineages*, 26).

CHAPTER THREE

Egyptian Cinema in a Transnational Context: Neoliberalism and Palestine Solidarity Cinema

In the three decades preceding the release of Egyptian director Yousry Nasrallah's two-part film about the Nakba, *Bab al-Shams* [*Gate of the Sun*] (2004), two peace agreements changed the course of Egyptian and Palestinian politics and relations. Under the presidency of Anwar El Sadat, who quickly instituted a set of neoliberal reforms known as the *infitah* (open door), Egypt became the first Arab state to forge diplomatic ties and economic cooperation with Israel at the 1978 Camp David Accords, to the dismay of Palestinians and much of the Arab world. This first step in the region toward normalization with the Zionist occupation entailed political, economic as well as cultural dimensions,[1] and paved the way for a lengthier "peace process," culminating in the infamous Oslo Accords in 1993/5. Signed as a bilateral agreement between the PLO and Israel, the Oslo Accords inaugurated a new political chapter in the Palestinian struggle, promising "limited autonomy" for Palestinians living inside the Occupied Territories, under the Palestinian Authority (PA). Yet decisions on the central issues of sovereignty, settlements, borders, Jerusalem and refugees were to be postponed to "final status" negotiations[2] with Israel ultimately retaining control over the Palestinian territories. This it did by instituting a "policy of closure,"[3] ruthlessly expanding its colonial settlements and continuing to bar the Palestinian diaspora from returning to their homes and properties through the promulgation of Judeo-centric laws such as the Law of Return and the Absentees' Property Law, 5710–1950, both passed in 1950.

As a result, a majority of Palestinians were forced to endure a protracted refugee status in the neighboring countries of Lebanon, Jordan and Syria.

As a consequence of this process of Egyptian integration into the global neoliberal order through a negotiated opening onto transnational capital flows, the marginalization, fragmentation and exploitation of Palestinians was exacerbated. At the same time, the increasingly organized Palestinian national resistance movement at no point stagnated or passively accepted their oppression within the unjust status quo. Rather, with the PLO shifting its base to Lebanon and the Palestinian refugee camps located there by the 1970s, Palestine's lengthy history of popular struggle would enter a next stage in the context of the fifteen year-long Lebanese Civil War (1975–90), essentially a proxy war fought between Israel and the PLO over the Palestinian question against the complex backdrop of Lebanon's sectarian political system.[4] Centered specifically around the Palestinian diaspora in Lebanon, with an eye to its political and geographical origins, *Gate of the Sun*—an adaptation of Lebanese author Elias Khoury's (1998) meticulously researched testimonial novel of the same name—traces the Nakba on to the Shatila refugee camp in Beirut during the mid-1990s.

Not unlike *The Dupes* (1972), *Gate of the Sun* blurs typical conceptions of a "national" Egyptian mode of cinematic production. Co-funded by Misr International, Youssef Chahine's production company based in Egypt, and the French-German public television channel, ARTE, which was launched in the early 1990s,[5] *Gate of the Sun* more properly represents the idea and practice of transnational cinematic production. Yet while Saleh's unsuccessful attempts to produce the pan-Arabist *The Dupes* in post-1967 Egypt compelled him to turn to the Syrian state for funding, Yousry Nasrallah—who was active in the 1970s student movement and the Egyptian Communist Workers Party,[6] and who graduated from the Cairo Higher of Institute of Cinema—would acquire partial funding for *Gate of the Sun* further afield, in Europe. With the consolidation of neoliberal globalization efforts by the 1990s, transnational co-productions had become an increasingly common phenomenon, oftentimes deemed a necessity on account of the economic dependency relationships produced between Western and "developing" countries by international institutions such as the IMF and World Bank.[7] The implementation of the Egyptian *infitah* came hand-in-hand with the normalization of Zionism, with loans and arms sales becoming contingent upon economic and geopolitical alliances with governments either in good standing with the Israeli state, such as France, Germany, and Saudi Arabia, or for which Israel was effectively a proxy state, namely the United States.

Egypt's 1978 peace treaty with Israel unsurprisingly rendered the depiction of Palestine and Palestinians in Egyptian cinema more difficult and controversial than ever. And yet *Gate of the Sun*, produced two decades after Camp David, is testament to the fact that the unresolved Palestinian question still retained critical importance for the Arab left intelligentsia, notwithstanding the retreat of radical Arab nationalist support for Palestine following the Defeat, and the harsh blow dealt by Camp David to the cause of Palestinian liberation. Deviating somewhat from official expressions of outrage directed at Egypt by other Arab member states of the Arab League—leading, for instance, to Egypt's temporary suspension from the Arab League and the boycott of Egyptian products—Egyptian intellectuals and artists would spearhead a cultural "Arab boycott" that was simultaneously critical of Egypt's normalization of relations with Israel and its embrace of *infitah*.[8] These dissenters stood, in solidarity with a struggle they understood to be integrally tied to their own, against political repression and capital accumulation.[9]

The generation of filmmakers to emerge from the student movement of this period, and whose first films would appear during the early 1980s, would come to be referred to, collectively, as the "New Realists."[10] While some New Realists took advantage of streams of Gulf capital then newly disposable for film production, others such as Yousry Nasrallah and Asma al-Bakri— who belonged to the generation of filmmakers following the New Realists that became prolific during the 1990s[11]—instead sought co-production arrangements with governmental entities such as France and European Union cultural agencies.[12] Indeed, exemplifying an anti-normalization ethos, Nasrallah's politics extended to funding choices. He was skeptical of the propagandistic and largely commercial interests of the increasingly hegemonic Gulf powers—another symptom of the *infitah*. Known for challenging social norms and broaching politically sensitive topics such as radical leftism and political Islam, Nasrallah saw more appeal in French funding and the aesthetic freedom it ostensibly provided.[13] (Of course, the politics of film funding are never neutral, and production support coming from Europe has also entailed stipulations, such as requisite appeal to liberal Western tastes and expectations, cultivated on the international film festival circuit.)

Indeed, by the 1990s, Egyptian cinema was becoming increasingly transnational, not only in the area of production but also—as *Gate of the Sun* exemplifies—in its circulation and reception. The global proliferation of television from the 1980s played a key role in this respect. European television channels such as ARTE and Canal+ began to provide new sources of funding and venues for broadcasting alternative films that would cater to the promotion of diasporic cultural identities.[14] With Egypt's embrace of neoliberalism and diplomatic rapprochement with Israel now extending to official media campaigns,[15] the question arose of how artists critical of those policies could navigate Egypt's transnationalizing political economy in order to draw attention to the Palestinian struggle. What aesthetic modalities and narrative forms might now be deployed for the purposes of forging cinematic solidarity with Palestine? *Gate of the Sun* was an exemplary response to this challenge, first in terms of its collaborative mode of production, and second through its self-reflexive, dialogic narrative structure that blends transnational cinema tropes with traditional storytelling techniques to produce a counter-hegemonic, polyphonic, oral history of the Nakba from the perspective of the film's contemporary present.

Egypt's Turn to Neoliberalism and Normalization of Israel: The Beginning of the "Peace Process"

Following the Defeat and Nasser's sudden death in 1970, Anwar El Sadat's subsequent Egyptian administration sought a reactionary change in economic structure and foreign policy. This turn back to capitalism had crucial implications for Palestine. The 1973 October War[16]—a fourth Arab–Israeli war that erupted after several years of protracted hostilities with Israel since 1967 and involved Egypt's attempts to regain the Sinai Peninsula from Israeli occupation—represents a particularly significant event in this context, in that it served to legitimate Sadat's rise to power and paved the way for Egypt's rapprochement with the United States and, five years later, Israel. In 1971, Sadat marked his departure from Nasser's non-aligned, pro-socialist track by launching a "Corrective Movement" that entailed purging Nasserist officials, imprisoning leftists, and expelling Soviet advisors.[17] Economically, Sadat (as well as his successor, Mubarak) worked to dismantle Nasser's public sector by promoting state deregulation, privatization and free trade in alignment with a globally emergent "neoliberal phase of capitalism."[18]

The effects and purported benefits of this neoliberalization effort, which included a partial re-privatization of the Egyptian film industry in 1971,[19] were unevenly felt: Egypt's "opening" to the West cultivated a transnationally-oriented consumer class of *nouveaux riches*, while Nasser's social pact, which had ensured basic needs for the working classes, rural peasants, and students, was broken.[20] When, in January 1977, Sadat announced drastic cuts to state subsidies, as per the World Bank and IMF's mandated recommendations for the reduction of Egyptian debt incurred by loans it had received from those key neoliberal funding sources, the working poor rose up in "bread riots" across Egyptian cities.[21] As a result, the state retaliated in a targeted campaign against the "remnants of the Egyptian nationalist and Marxist left."[22]

Significant ideological changes occurred in turn within the upper ranks of the Egyptian political system, including especially those spearheaded by the rise of political Islam. The Muslim Brotherhood, in existence since the pre-Nasser period and largely suppressed under Nasser, began to gain power and visibility because, as investors in commercial capital (via trade with the Gulf countries), its members benefited materially from the neoliberal project.[23] State-owned Egyptian assets were sold not only to senior officers and high government officials but also to businessmen, many of them Brotherhood members returning from the Gulf countries. Indeed, the Sadat administration began to foster a symbiotic economic relationship with Saudi Arabia and other oil-producing states in the Gulf region, whereby Egyptian labor could be exchanged for oil wealth.[24] Hence the vast increase in labor migration and proliferation of migrant networks between the Gulf and other Arab states, with many Palestinians, too—as foreshadowed in *The Dupes*—moving to countries like Kuwait and Iraq for work. The ensuing growth of Gulf capital also affected the cinema industry, whereby Egyptian films produced with Gulf money, primarily to fill a gap in the Saudi market for cinema, were given the moniker *sinima al-muqawalat* (contractors or entrepreneur cinema) and quickly derided as low-value.[25]

Egypt's turn to neoliberalism became a cornerstone of its dealings with Palestine/Israel and necessitated a paradigm shift in the official narrative, not least considering the popular support for the Palestinian struggle which had been cultivated under Nasser. The Egyptian media was instrumentalized as part of an "information effort" to blame Egypt's growing economic hardships on the state's lengthy and, by implication, costly involvement in the Palestinian struggle. It launched a large-scale celebration of Sadat's rise to power and framed the 1973 October War, over which he presided, as an out-and-out success—and, by extension, a closing chapter in Egypt's hostilities against Israel—partially in order to deflect attention from the IMF debt which had already begun to accrue and lower living standards for the masses of Egyptians. This media effort served effectively to attract popular support for the peace treaty with Israel a few years later, when Sadat's visit to Jerusalem in 1977 to demand Israeli withdrawal from the Sinai Peninsula set the Camp David negotiations into motion.[26]

Undeniably, the most significant development in Egyptian–Palestinian relations of the 1970s, with effects that were long to outlive that turbulent decade, the agreement negotiated between Sadat and his U.S. and Israeli counterparts at Camp David stipulated that in return for the Sinai, Egypt would acknowledge the Zionist entity as a sovereign, Israeli state. For Egypt, full recognition of Israel brought debt write-offs and military aid from the United States[27] and would form a new pillar of Egyptian foreign policy that would be upheld into the new century, when *Gate of the Sun* was produced. Although sometimes uncritically heralded as the Middle East's greatest peace breakthrough, this first of a series of "peace agreements" (followed by the 1991 Madrid conference co-sponsored by the United States and the nearly defunct Soviet Union) leading up to the 1993/5 Oslo Accords had damaging repercussions for the future of the Palestinian liberation struggle as well as for the balance of power across the Arab region.

The Camp David peace treaty was widely opposed throughout the Arab world and within the Egyptian populace.[28] Whereas the PLO and states nominally more supportive of the PLO such as Syria, Iraq, Libya, and Algeria were angered by Egypt having struck a deal with the enemy, thus capitulating to Israeli expansionism, Jordan and Saudi Arabia criticized the agreement more moderately. Egypt was expelled from the Arab League (only to be readmitted in 1989), the headquarters of which was moved from Cairo to Tunis, where the PLO was also then headquartered after its expulsion from Lebanon in 1982.[29] The Arab League also decided to impose economic sanctions against Egypt,[30] employing an Arab boycott strategy with origins dating back to the late 1940s, when it was initially waged against Israel.[31] This official boycott extended to Egyptian cinema, which until that time comprised the region's most widely disseminated popular media: Egyptian films were temporarily prohibited distribution and exhibition in Arab League member states, with Egyptian film industry production stagnating as a result.[32] The most vocal opposition within Egypt, both to *infitah* and cultural normalization, emanated from the left intelligentsia and activists who, from the onset, criticized Camp David's relinquishing of Egyptian sovereignty to neocolonial entities, thus permitting the expansion of Israeli and U.S. power across the region.[33] Such domestic civil society opposition, which saw the peace treaty with Israel as a sellout to U.S.-backed capital, gained strength throughout the Arab world during the 1970s and 1980s, prompting Egyptian public expressions of support for the Palestinian resistance and a radical anti-normalization campaign. If Camp David had hindered Egyptian diplomats from confronting Israel, the Egyptian intelligentsia were in a unique position to refuse cooperation with aspects of the peace treaty that fell outside the purview of diplomats and politicians. The Committee for the Defense of the Arab National Culture in Egypt, for instance, pushed for a cultural boycott that included protesting the participation of Israel in Cairo's annual Book Fair in the early 1980s.[34] As for Egyptian films, which until that time comprised the region's most widely disseminated popular media, they were temporarily prohibited distribution and exhibition in Arab League member states, with Egyptian film industry production stagnating as a result.[35]

The Palestinian National Movement and Diaspora in (Post-)1970s Lebanon

The Six-Day War that resulted in the Israeli occupation of the Palestinian West Bank and Gaza, the Egyptian Sinai Peninsula and the Syrian Golan Heights / al-Jawlan signaled the eclipse of Nasser's state-led nationalist support for the Palestinian struggle under the rubric of his particular configuration of pan-Arabism. In response to this gradual retreat, Palestinian armed struggle, which had begun to cohere in refugee camps throughout the preceding decade, emerged as a preferred, more direct strategy of *muqawamah* (resistance) and national liberation. The base of the Palestinian guerilla effort was initially cultivated in and around Amman, Jordan following the Israeli takeover of the Jordan-controlled West Bank in 1967 but was soon forced to relocate to Lebanon, in the wake of the brutal Black September events in 1970,[36] where it would resume activities. Throughout the 1970s, Lebanon thus became the central hub for the Palestinian resistance, whereby the PLO—in alliance with the Lebanese National Movement—transformed South Lebanon and its Palestinian refugee camps into a zone of militant liberation struggle.[37] By the mid-1970s, the PLO had managed to win United Nations and Arab League recognition as the primary representative of the Palestinian people, a negotiated development that would gradually pave the way for the ensuing diplomatic "solutions" to the Palestinian struggle beginning with Camp David.[38]

The refugee camps, which came under Palestinian jurisdiction as "quasi-liberated zones" of the Palestinian revolution,[39] had originally been set up after the Nakba by the United Nations Relief and Works Agency (UNRWA) in order to accommodate displaced Palestinians from the Galilee region. The Shatila refugee camp featured in *Gate of the Sun* was established in 1949 outside Beirut, and Mieh Mieh, which also appears in the film, was established in 1954, south of the Lebanese city of Saida. UNRWA and the Lebanese government came to constitute the primary "apparatus of governance" for Palestinian refugees in Lebanon. As per the 1969 Cairo Agreement, Palestinians in Lebanon were granted the right to engage in armed struggle as well as work in Lebanon, although in practice, employment outside the camps was rarely permitted—at least not for most Muslim Palestinians.[40] The majority of Palestinian refugees were excluded from all public and many private areas of employment, for which they had nonetheless to apply for work permits.[41] The sectarian Lebanese government, always unstable since the time of its postcolonial formation, was concerned that a large pool of low-wage foreign labor would lead to popular uprisings,[42] and perhaps that the economic support which sustained employment could bring to Palestinians would raise the ire of the militarily superior Israeli state.

Indeed, Lebanon's sectarian government has taken an historically ambivalent posture regarding the Palestinian refugees and, during the 1970s, regarding the PLO's armed presence on the outskirts of Beirut and Saida. With the government's political representation and distribution of resources apportioned by sect (including Maronite Christians, Sunni Muslims, Shi'a Muslims, Greek Orthodox and Druze communities), the Lebanese authorities perceived the Sunni-majority Palestinians as a threat to their fragile political system.[43] During the Lebanese Civil War, the Palestinian refugee camps came increasingly under fire from the Lebanese army, right-wing Christian militias (the Maronite Phalangists and the Chamounists), and frequent Israeli incursions.[44] The 1982 Israeli invasion of Lebanon had particularly deleterious implications for the Palestinian refugees, leading to yet another expulsion of the PLO—this time to Tunis. Neither the United States nor Lebanon honored its commitment to guarantee protection and safety to the Palestinians subsequently left behind in the refugee camps.[45]

Palestinians living in Lebanese refugee camps have frequently referred to themselves as "the forgotten people" due to their inhospitable living conditions and the fact that they are strictly denied Lebanese citizenship.[46] Such confinement and limitations notwithstanding, Palestinians have never accepted their refugee status, nor have they remained inactive against it. A crucial phase in the political, economic and social development of the Palestinian diaspora, the 1970s was the decade in which the PLO set up and developed a range of civil and service institutions, "gave specificity and coherence to the Palestinian political cause (…) and placed the Palestinians and the Palestine question on the international political agenda."[47] With good reason, terms such as *sumoud* (steadfastness), *muqawamah* (resistance), *haqq al-awda* (right of return) have over time permeated everyday language and symbolic practices in the camps.[48] Non-violent *sumoud* was soon accompanied by more demonstrative resistance during the First Intifada that swept across the West Bank and Gaza in 1987, triggered by everyday frustrations over life under oppressive military occupation, the proliferation of Jewish-only Israeli settlements, and the ineffective leadership of the PLO in Tunis.[49] Although the Intifada attracted worldwide attention as a vital spark in the Palestinian struggle, its roots go back to the earliest stages of the Zionist colonization of historic Palestine—a lengthier history of which *Gate of the Sun* makes a point to trace. For this reason, the First Intifada was not really the first such Palestinian uprising, although it served, among other things, as an important reminder of the organized nature of Palestinian resistance, which by this point had "extensive experience of clandestine activity."[50]

An attempt to contain the revolutionary fervor revivified by the First Intifada came a few years later in the form of the 1993/5 Oslo Accords. This agreement between Israel and the PLO led to the PLO's move from Tunisia to Palestine/Israel and the establishment of the Palestinian Authority (PA), a governing body which was granted limited self-rule over the Palestinian population in the West Bank and Gaza Strip.[51] Effectively intended to build "trust" between Palestinians and Israelis, the Oslo Accords' most immediate effect on Palestinians was in fact their increased separation, and political division, through the ensuing Israeli policy of enclosure.[52] Worse even for the Palestinian diaspora, the Oslo agreements made no mention of the internationally mandated right of the refugees to return home—an elision which Palestinians across the diaspora saw as a fundamental betrayal on the part of their leadership.[53] Meanwhile, popular mobilization for Palestine in neighboring Egypt accumulated and surged in the wake of events such as the Israeli invasion of Lebanon in 1982, the Second ("Al-Aqsa") Intifada in 2000, and the US-led invasion of Iraq in 2003. Indeed, a range of groups, including leftists, Nasserists and young Muslim Brotherhood members, soon formed the Egyptian Popular Committee in Solidarity with the Palestinian Intifada—"irrespective of political and historical differences."[54] As such, while Camp David and Oslo clearly gestured toward a more diplomatic turn in the Egypt–Palestine nexus, there is ample evidence of organized grassroots and popular struggle against Zionist hegemony within both populations, and—as the rest of this chapter argues—*Gate of the Sun* represents a serious attempt to grapple cinematically with these challenges.

Memory and Return: Intergenerational Dialogue as Counter-hegemonic Representation

Divided into two parts entitled "The Departure" and "The Return," *Gate of the Sun* weaves a collection of Palestinian histories, memories and testimonies into an epic, four and one-half hour narrative that spans the pre-Nakba days to the Oslo period. While violent scenes of village expulsions, exodus-like processions across the hilly Galilean landscape, and re-enacted footage of Palestinian resettlement punctuate the first part of the film, which looks back to the onset of the Nakba, the second half centers around its ongoing effects on the subsequent generation of Palestinians—specifically those living diasporically in the Shatila refugee camp. The two parts are strung together by a frame story set in a camp hospital—the setting of the film's diegetic present tense—and narrated by Khalil (Bassel Khayyat), a nurse and former PLO guerilla fighter during the Lebanese Civil War, whose symbolic role as a solidarity figure and narrator mediating Palestinian generations is noteworthy. As he keeps vigil at the bedside of a comatose patient who is also his father-figure, Younes (Orwa Nyrabia), Khalil recounts Younes's memories of both the Nakba and his heroic participation in the Palestinian armed resistance, attempting to talk him back to consciousness and thus keep him alive. The film's title denotes a cave called Bab al-Shams that occupies a central place in Younes' story; located near his home village in the Galilee, it is the site where—as we learn through several flashbacks—he would secretly visit his lover, Nahila (Rim Turkhi), when returning from his guerilla activities in occupied Palestine to the Southern Lebanese hills. Their love story forms a metaphorical subplot throughout the film ("the homeland is like love"), the cave itself carrying symbolic resonance as an intimate reservoir of shared stories and dreams—a sacred Palestinian space which, it is implied, will outlive the film's ending.

Gate of the Sun's dialogic structure renders an intricate interplay between past and present, aptly allegorizing lived reality for the exiled Palestinian population who reside at a spatiotemporal distance from the homeland. With their respective master narratives, relationships to, and modes of knowledgeability regarding Palestine, Younes and Khalil epitomize two paradigmatic generations of Palestinians: the 1948 generation, with its memories of the Nakba directly witnessed, and the post-1967, diasporic generation that grew up abroad and learned about Palestine through stories transmitted by their elders. The narrative strands represented by these two generations overlap and branch out into many more, producing a polyphonic oral history about the loss of Palestine and its enduring aftermath in which reflexively staged acts of telling, remembering, and

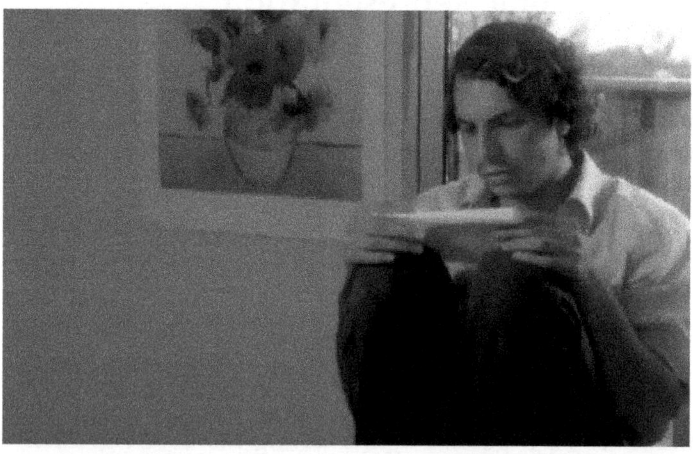

Figure 3.1 *Gate of the Sun* [*Bab al-Shams*] (Yousry Nasrallah, Egypt/France, 2004).

listening become as significant as the multiple (hi)stories themselves. For instance, as Khalil dialogues with his unconscious patient shots are interspersed in which Khalil appears to address the camera directly with an urgent sense of responsibility, thus constructing a collective subjectivity into which the spectator is loosely sutured. This "epistolary" tendency, a mode of narrativity that is "structurally political, critical, and counterhegemonic"[55] and constitutes a common trope of transnational and diasporic cinema, appears in various guises throughout the film.

As Hamid Naficy (2001) has extensively theorized, diasporic narratives are often driven by "a burning desire to know and to tell about the causes, experiences, and consequences of disrupted personal and national histories."[56] A letter which Khalil receives from his mother Najwa, who lives in the West Bank city of Ramallah, containing a telephone number that he is ironically able to call only from a borrowed French mobile phone, constitutes another, exemplary epistolary device that facilitates the narrative's play with distance and proximity while also critiquing Israeli policies of enclosure, including control of telecommunications, which have separated Palestinian communities within and across borders since Oslo. As Khalil explains to the slightly tacky, albeit good-willed French actress who visits the Shatila camp for a day while in Beirut to research the production of a play by the French author and activist Jean Genet: "That is the Palestinian diaspora. I am not allowed to go to Palestine without an Israeli permit." Although "The Departure" and "The Return" would seem to evoke a conventional narrative trajectory that in this case is circular, *Gate of the Sun* expressly rejects an authoritative voice, clear telos or straightforward (re)solution; the journey it traces is in fact dialectical. Elias Khoury explains his artistic choice: "*Gate of the Sun* is an unfinished novel, and it will remain open until the moment when this wound is healed."[57] The film similarly enacts the unresolved Palestinian struggle by foregrounding the diaspora stuck in limbo, waiting to return, and concludes with an anti-climactic scene of return set in the post-Oslo 1990s. In what is set up to serve as a kind of farewell, the cave in this scene—no longer the safe haven regularly revisited—is sealed and left behind, with Nahila's voice-over proclaiming Bab al-Shams "the only liberated land left in Palestine which no Israeli has entered." After her children are shown fetching Younes' and her possessions from the cave, a subsequent shot from inside the dark space captures three young men carrying fully laden bags out into the sunlight. "I asked them not to open it again until their grandfather returns," Nahila's voice-over continues, filling the space with a simultaneous sense of pastness and precarity. This staging of Bab al-Shams' closure in the final scene allegorizes the responsibility conferred upon subsequent Palestinian generations to safeguard and preserve Palestine.

While no *real* return to Palestine occurs in *Gate of the Sun*, the notion of return nonetheless emerges as a shared Palestinian longing that is staged repeatedly through storytelling. Calls for return to the homeland manifest in the frequently exclaimed "min al-awwal!" (from the beginning!), which recalls the popular "kan ya makan" (once upon a time) of Arab storytelling tradition—for example, that of Scheherazade[58] in *Alf Layla wa Layla* (*One Thousand and One Nights*). Early in "The Departure," for instance, Khalil tells his unconscious patient: "Let us start from the beginning. At the beginning there was Palestine." As his voice-over continues, the camera drifts slowly from the hospital room onto its balcony, before a fade-in to a panoramic, hilly landscape—briefly overlaid with the intertitle, "Galilee 1945"—resituates the plot almost 50 years into the past. The ensuing visual projection of Younes' memories of his Galilean home village of 'Ayn al-Zaytoun, initially framed by Khalil's narration, is soon synchronized with the visualized memories of multiple other characters who also experienced the violent rupture of the Nakba and whose perspectives are likewise figured within Khalil's narratological framing.

A more realist aesthetic is employed in much of the film's second half. Here the narrative alternates between the diegetic present tense of the refugee camp and the diegetic past tense of Khalil's framed storytelling, with its divergent and overlapping tangents leading to the contemporary 1990s. The temporal immediacy structuring this part of the film is made apparent when the camera cranes away from the hospital balcony to capture a lively resistance march taking place on the streets directly below. The flurry of colorful banners bearing slogans such as "Right of Return," alongside men, women and children chanting "No to Oslo—No to Madrid!," demonstrates Palestinian refugee opposition to Oslo and the subsequent "peace" agreements. Flashbacks to Khalil's activities as a guerilla fighter in the Lebanese mountains as well as to a training trip to China harken, in turn, to an earlier moment during the 1970s, when militant internationalism proposed a different kind of solution and vision for the Palestinians. In this instance, Khalil's voice-over states, "I became a *fedayee* when the whole world was a *fedayee*," and is paired with stills of international guerilla heroes such as Che Guevara, Ho Chi Minh, and Yasser Arafat.

The generational switch in perspective that here splits the film into two distinct, if at times overlapping, narratives is significant, in that it illustrates how memories and political imaginaries—and therefore also representations—of Palestine have changed over time, depending upon their respective conditions and historical relationship to the Nakba. While pre-Nakba rural life is regularly depicted in the film in an idyllic, melodramatic manner, with frequent long takes of the landscape and natural diegetic sound, it is typically interrupted by dramatized scenes of expulsion, the spatial enclosure and everyday life conditions in the Shatila camp encouraging a less idealized, more ad hoc view. The two parts of *Gate of the Sun* arguably correspond to two main chronotopes of exile, as elaborated by Naficy: "open- and closed-form aesthetics,"[59] which serve respectively to depict a remembered, imagined past, and the precarity and liminality of the present. Nasrallah himself explained that the film's structural duality is meant to avoid an ideological framing of Palestinian history; he wanted to place the two generalized historical perspectives, and their corresponding modes of representation, into dialectical relationship, with "The Return" constituting a response or "antithesis" to "The Departure"[60] rather than either standing exclusive of it or flowing seamlessly from it. Furthermore, the second part is in a way an attempt to articulate the disconnect and frustration felt by the more radicalized, post-1967 generation (to which both Yousry Nasrallah and Elias Khoury belonged), toward heroic, nationalist or pan-Arab master narratives about the past, as well as overly nostalgic conceptions of the pre-1948 period. This may also account for the element of ridicule that appears in the film's allusion to other Arab state actors, such as via the depiction of the Arab Liberation Army in 1948 (Part One) or in the form of an eccentric and comical Egyptian man shown running around the camp in Part Two—in both cases implying a lack of seriousness and efficacy. (The misfit Egyptian also figures in an earlier Egyptian film about Palestine—or, more accurately, about a Palestinian figure—New Realist director Atef El Tayeb's *Nagi al-Ali* (1991), starring popular Egyptian actor Nour el-Sharif in the lead role of the famous Palestinian cartoonist Naji al-Ali. In this film, a drunken, nameless Egyptian man asks Naji, during the Israeli invasion of Lebanon in 1982, "When will the Arab armies come?" to which Naji responds: "They're busy."[61])

Gate of the Sun's structural dialectic thus stands to critique a singular narratology in a way that is unlike the simplistic, chronological narratives of the patriotic Egyptian melodramas about the Palestine War, and is also distinct from *The Dupes*' temporally collocated subjectivities of failed Palestinian resistance in the years preceding the Naksa.[62] Instead by mediating generational temporalities, *Gate of the Sun* at once displays fragmented histories and commits to preserving a range of Palestinian memories—of a struggle that is ongoing. In so doing, the film also compels its spectator to face up to the challenges of narrativizing Palestine. Both memory and return serve as central themes bearing distinct and multilayered temporalities that, through their critical intersectionality, allegorize the unacceptability of persistently deferring a just resolution to the Palestinian issue.

Critical Aesthetics of Solidarity: Collaborative Authorship and Counter-memory

In addition to being the product of a transnational cultural collaboration between an Egyptian film production company and a French television channel, *Gate of the Sun* is also the product of a collaboration organized by a group of Arab leftist artists whose pathways converged in Beirut during the Lebanese Civil War. At this crucial post-1967 conjuncture, Beirut became a "radical intellectual and literary node," with dissident Egyptians, among others, moving there from Cairo, where they ended up working as editors for leftist newspapers and magazines and became involved in Palestine solidarity activism.[63] *Gate of the Sun* is a case in point of this alliance between radical authorship and Palestine solidarity, in that both Nasrallah and the film's screenwriter, Lebanese independent filmmaker Mohamed Soueid, worked as journalists and film critics for the leftist pro-Palestine Lebanese newspaper *As-Safir* from the late 1970s into the 1980s.[64] Elias Khoury was in turn the editor of the journal *Shu'un Filastinia* (*Palestinian Affairs*) from 1975 to 1979, in collaboration with prominent Palestinian poet Mahmoud Darwish. This milieu also saw the emergence of Palestinian oral history projects, with Khoury himself collecting many testimonies in the process of researching the conditions of Palestinian refugees in Lebanon for his book. As he relates,

> My personal relationship with the [N]akba began through the long process of work on my novel *Gate of the Sun* (…) I felt that my job was to collect memories and write stories never written before. In this huge personal journey, I discovered Palestine, a land I had never visited.[65]

Moving from the extra-textual to the onscreen features of *Gate of the Sun*, it is possible to conceive of Khalil's figure itself as a kind of testimony collector and storyteller—one who enacts the solidary practice of oral history narration and preservation. Comparable to the film's collaborative authorship, Khalil stands in an indirect yet committed relationship to Palestine, someone who retells history from the lived reality of the Lebanese Civil War, unable to visit, much less return to, Palestine. He embodies a liminal position mediating the 1948 and post-1967 generations, between the inside and outside of Palestine—but also between the diegetic and the extra-textual—through his nuanced address of the spectator.

Toward the end of the film, for instance, Khalil is depicted walking back to his unadorned home in the Shatila camp, while, in his ongoing imaginary dialogue with unconscious Younis, he broaches the topic of Nahila's death: "Nahila died, and you are on the way to dying. But don't die like this." The ambiguity of second person address means that the "you" here could refer both to the older generation of Palestinians and to the attentive spectator or even to a broader collectivity. After a cut to the inside of a dark room, the camera captures Khalil entering: "Do you want other stories?" he asks, standing in the dimly lit threshold. "I don't have any more. It's over." Walking closer to the camera, he adds, "Enough talking," before directly facing the camera: "Between your history and mine, I'm lost." This shot of Khalil at the threshold, explicating his dilemma, is followed by a cut to a black-and-white photograph of Nahila, her village pictured in the background, in which she appears to be looking directly at him and the camera before the camera comes to hover over multiple other snapshots of a forcefully fragmented family, each image pinned to the wall. This scene, much like several similarly contemplative, threshold moments throughout *Gate of the Sun*, strikingly emanates from Khalil's in-between position as a signifier of the Palestinian diaspora that situates him within a space of affective, filial attachment to a tangibly inaccessible historic Palestine. In this context, and by way of Younis, Khalil searches for his personal history too, which includes struggling to recapture an image of his actual father whom he had lost during childhood. The film's meta-reflexive questioning of what it means to remember, to historicize—or, as this book asks more generally, to cinematically "represent"—the Nakba, runs throughout the frame story.

The post-1967 Arab left also belonged to a generation that was skeptical of the heroic nationalism and grand narratives associated with the promises held up by Younis' generation. A similar critique is projected by life-long refugee Khalil. A key characteristic ascribed by Nur Masalha (2018) to oral history projects is their emphasis on "histories from below," their prioritization of the voices and perspectives of refugees, peasants and women over official, patriarchal and elite histories.[66] *Gate of the Sun* takes a clear step in that direction. In addition to demonstrating solidarity with the Palestinian diaspora in Lebanon, the film also sides with and centers the emancipatory struggles of Palestinian women across the generations. The trajectories of Younis' lover Nahila and Khalil's lover Shams undergo an evident process of transformation, lending the film a feminist undertone. While the film does not shy away from depicting Shams' traditional village wedding, in which she participates at the fragile age of 15, in the first half of the film, the personal history she shares with Khalil at a later point maps an increasingly autonomous, militant geography that allegorizes the journey of the Palestinian resistance from Amman to Tel El Zaatar back to Jordan followed by Tripoli—when she herself would join the Palestinian resistance.

Nahila in turn follows a similarly emancipatory trajectory, as *Gate of the Sun* critically resituates her role from that of a listener to that of a storyteller. In the first part of the film, Nahila and the other peasant women are portrayed as bound by tradition, oftentimes unwillingly so. Here the film resists casting a victimizing gaze, as the camera reflexively re-centers the women so as to unsettle the spectator, who is made to witness young Nahila's subjugation by patriarchal imperatives and rationales. In the pre-1948 Galilean village context represented toward the beginning of the film, the camera pans from the village school insignia, "Ayn al-Zaytoun," to a classroom window into which a woman is shown peering. Inside, a male teacher can be seen pointing to a hand-drawn map of Palestine, which he uses to instruct his pupils, whom he asks to repeat in unison: "This is the map of?"—"Palestine!" At this point the camera starts to follow the woman as she walks to a second window and continues to watch the history lesson unfold. The teacher explains that the Zionists want to occupy all of Palestine and "chase us away." He circles areas on the map to clarify for his pupils what is meant. A cut to a longer shot then reveals that Nahila is the woman looking in, and an even longer shot subsequently portrays multiple women, who are positioned across several planes of the mise-en-scene, peering over at the school. This series of shots makes for a striking commentary on the women's exclusion from the didactic schoolroom notwithstanding their eager attentiveness to the lesson.[67]

In "The Return," *Gate of the Sun*'s dialectical structure again becomes a means of projecting a counter-narrative. Nahila confronts Younes in Bab al-Shams after he proudly tells her about his activities as a *fedayee* at the border between Lebanon and occupied Palestine: "You know, passing the Israeli frontier is a real battle: *Fedayeen* at the borders, guerilla operations, and I'm the responsible for the military sector." The camera then cuts to Nahila, who proclaims: "I know, but today I'm not listening to you. I'm speaking. I want to speak, listen to me." As her demanding voice continues into voice-over format, a cut to the exterior of the

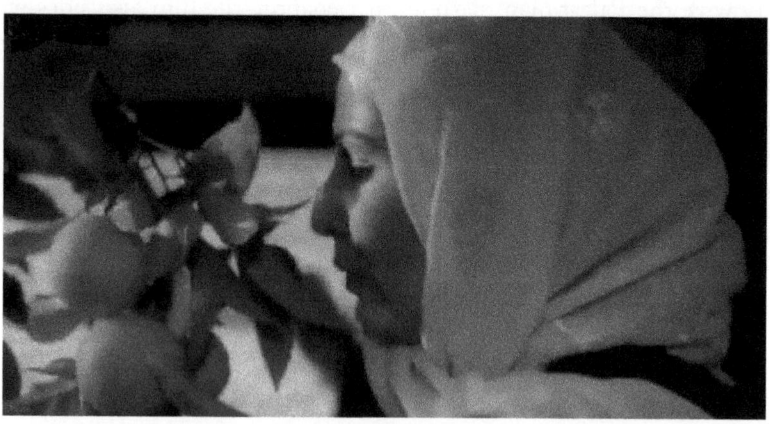

Figure 3.2 *Gate of the Sun* [*Bab al-Shams*] (Yousry Nasrallah, Egypt/France, 2004).

cave—the camera moving through the trees in the dark—allows the conversation to continue within a more generalized context, at which point Nahila's tone of voice turns more pressing: "You don't know anything. You think that the mountains you cross are everything in life—but who am I? Do you know who we are?" Now looking directly looking into the camera, Nahila in the next shot states assertively, "Don't misunderstand me"—before proudly telling her lover about her response to an Israeli officer who had confronted her one day in the village: "I told them we aren't Arabs—we are Palestinians," she says after lamenting how Lebanese, Syrians and Egyptians get to claim their nationality, whereas Palestinians often get subsumed under the general category, "Arabs." Her remark resonates with the Palestinian dissatisfaction with controlled pan-Arabism (discussed in Chapter Two), in addition to highlighting the common Israeli practice of denying the existence of Palestinians by using the term *Arab* instead. A subsequent statement, directed at Younes, suggests Nahila's frustration with masculinist national narratives, to which she has been forced to listen: "You came with your histories of Saladin and Nasser, and I believed you. You filled Bab al-Shams with heroic epics." Nahila's emphasis on a Palestinian counter-memory[68] testifies to a more far-reaching Palestinian desire no longer to be spoken for, (mis)represented or molded to fit someone else's cause. The transformation of Nahila—a synecdoche of Palestinian women—from listener to *acteur* positions women as the emblematic heroes of the Palestinian struggle, distinctly aware of the everyday realities of protracted exile and ever-encroaching normalization, as exemplified by Nahila's wry comment concerning Palestinian children who "now speak Hebrew better than the Jews." In short, *Gate of the Sun*'s inscription of counter-memory demonstrates, as Humphries and Khalili (2007) succinctly put it, that

> Women have had a seldom-acknowledged role as conduits of Nakba memory. Though often silenced and circumscribed by multiple dominant discourses, they have promulgated concrete narratives and details about life in Palestine and the dislocation and losses of the Nakba across generations. Their narratives, at the very least, complicate and extend better-known histories and memories about the Nakba.[69]

In this respect, *Gate of the Sun*'s female counter-mnemonic structuring lends the film an intersectional quality that in turn critically allegorizes the increasingly transnational production conditions which had gained a foothold in Egyptian cinema during the latter decades of the twentieth century. Symptomatic of these transnational, globalized conditions is an acceleration of border-crossings, leading to increased cultural hybridity and prompting an understanding of cultural positionalities in their interconnectedness. The film's range of themes and intertextual references associated with Palestine, the Nakba and the Palestinian diaspora are cumulative signs of a liberation struggle that is more than one-half century old, that shows little sign of ending, but whose scope has widened to include populations and struggles previously marginalized within the dominant movement. The sustained and repeated presence of such references in *Gate of the Sun* gestures to the ongoing and unresolved nature of the Palestinian issue, its growing historicity, its multigenerational dynamic and multi-sited geographies. At the same time, the film is symptomatic of a distinct moment in the historical and technological development of Egyptian cinema, with its multiple intertextual references to earlier aesthetic traditions and generic conventions. As Ginsberg (2016) argues in her analysis of the film: "*Gate of the Sun*, (…) not unlike other films Nasrallah has directed, participates in the prevailing integration of realism and melodrama while politicizing them explicitly in several respects."[70] Indeed, *Gate of the Sun* draws upon a rich repertoire of cinematic tropes and aesthetic styles familiar from Egyptian, Palestinian and transnational cinema, creatively repurposing melodrama, with its affective and mythical capacities, while also including attributes of documentary such as the gritty realism that we see in the refugee camp scenes and various talking heads segments, to fit—and challenge—the sensibilities of the transnational moment.

Granted its contemporary context, by which point the gradual normalization of the Israeli presence in the region, the retreat of the militant internationalism which had promised more radical support for Palestine, and the rapid spread of neoliberalism had come to overdetermine Egypt's role in the Palestinian struggle, we must consider *Gate of the Sun*—its commitment to preserving historical memory and to redirecting attention to the Palestinian diaspora and its right of return—all the more urgent, and an important counter-narrative within the annals of Egyptian cinema.

Notes

1 Barbara Harlow, "Egyptian Intellectuals and the Debate on the 'Normalization of Cultural Relations,'" *Cultural Critique*, no. 4 (1986): 37.

2 Samih K. Farsoun and Christina Zacharia Hawatmeh, *Palestine and the Palestinians* (Boulder: Westview Press, 1997), 209.

3 The policy of closure represents "the defining economic feature of the post-Oslo period." Not only has this sealing off of the Palestinian Occupied Territories from Israel and from other external markets "proved extremely damaging to the Palestinian economy, particularly labor and trade," it has also "resulted in two new processes: growing economic 'enclavization' and emerging economic autarky in an economy already weakened by de-development"

(Sara Roy, "De-Development Revisited: Palestinian Economy and Society Since Oslo," *Journal of Palestine Studies* 28, no. 3 (April 1999): 68).

4 See Fawwāz Ṭarābulsī, *A History of Modern Lebanon* (London and Ann Arbor, MI: Pluto Press, 2007), 109–27. See also Max Weiss, *In the Shadow of Sectarianism: Law, Shi'ism, and the Making of Modern Lebanon* (Cambridge, MA: Harvard University Press, 2010).

5 Benjamin Geer, "Yousry Nasrallah: The Pursuit of Autonomy in the Arab and European Film Markets (Egypt)," in *Ten Arab Filmmakers: Political Dissent and Social Critique*, ed. Josef Gugler (Bloomington: Indiana University Press, 2015), 144.

6 Geer, "Yousry Nasrallah," 145.

7 As Sean F. McMahon argues, "debt, the bringing of yet-to-be-produced future value into the present moment, either for states or the working class as consumers, is one way of temporally shifting capitalism's crisis tendencies. The process of privatization by which public goods are commodified and transformed into new sites of accumulation is another way to defer the crisis tendency" (McMahon, *Crisis and Class War in Egypt: Social Reproduction, Factional Realignments and the Global Political Economy* (London: Zed, 2017), 19). The United States, in particular, was set on linking its allies "into a single economic space, characterized by free trade and investment flows" (Adam Hanieh, *Lineages of Revolt: Issues of Contemporary Capitalism in the Middle East* (Chicago: Haymarket, 2013), 107).

8 See Elliott Colla, "Solidarity in the Time of Anti-Normalization," *Middle East Report*, no. 224 (2002): 11.

9 Reem Abou-El-Fadl, "The Road to Jerusalem through Tahrir Square: Anti-Zionism and Palestine in the 2011 Egyptian Revolution," *Journal of Palestine Studies* 41, no. 2 (January 2012): 7.

10 Significant directors from this movement include Atef El Tayeb *Sawwaq al-Utubis* (*Busdriver*, 1982), Mohamed Khan, *Zaugat Ragul Muhim* (*Wife of an Important Man*, 1987); Khairy Beshara, *Yom Murr, Yom Helw* (*Bitter Day, Sweet Day*, 1988), and Daoud Abd El-Sayyed, *KitKat* (1991).

11 Samir Farid, *Madkhal ila tarikh al-sinima al-'arabiya*. Cairo: Egyptian General Book Institute, 2001, 16.

12 Garay Menicucci, "Europe and the Political Economy of Arab Cinema," *Middle East Report*, no. 235 (Summer 2005): 46.

13 French financial support for Maghrebi cinema is not a recent phenomenon; it has been going on for a long time.
See Will Higbee, *Post-Beur Cinema: North African Emigre and Maghrebi-French Filmmaking in France since 2000* (Edinburgh: Edinburgh University Press, 2013); and Karim Tartoussieh, "Life Is Like a Bowl of Fish: *The Aquarium*, the French New Wave and the Urban Reflection of the Cairene Self," *Journal for Cultural Research* 16, no. 2–3 (July 2012): 289.

14 Hamid Naficy, *An Accented Cinema: Exilic and Diasporic Filmmaking* (Princeton, NJ: Princeton University Press, 2018), 44.

15 Ghada Hashem Talhami, *Palestine in the Egyptian Press: From Al-Ahram to Al-Ahali* (Lanham, MD: Lexington Books, 2007), 328–35.

16 Israel refers to this war as the Yom Kippur War, while in the Arab world it is known as the Ramadan War. Officially, the October War was celebrated as one of Egypt's most heroic military successes, boosting Sadat's image among the Egyptian populace. See Ewan Stein, *Representing Israel in Modern Egypt: Ideas, Intellectuals and Foreign Policy from Nasser to Mubarak*

(London: Bloomsbury Academic, 2012), 121. For critiques of this rhetoric, see Hazem Kandil, *Soldiers, Spies, and Statesmen: Egypt's Road to Revolt* (London and New York: Verso, 2014), 113–157.

17 Kandil, *Soldiers*, 99–111.

18 Hanieh, *Lineages*, 27.

19 Kay Dickinson, *Arab Film and Video Manifestos: Forty-Five Years of the Moving Image Amid Revolution* (Cham, Switzerland: Palgrave Macmillan, 2018), 45.

20 Hanieh, *Lineages*, 26.

21 McMahon, *Crisis and Class War*, 60.

22 Malek Khouri, *The Arab National Project in Youssef Chahine's Cinema* (Cairo: American University in Cairo Press, 2010), 115.

23 Sara Salem, *Anticolonial Afterlives in Egypt: The Politics of Hegemony* (Cambridge, UK: Cambridge University Press, 2020), 185.
See also McMahon's (2017) Marxist economic analysis of Egypt, which discusses how "the rise of 'Islamism' is dialectically related to the increasing aggressiveness of capital's neoliberal project." McMahon, *Crisis and Class War*, 87.

24 Hanieh, *Lineages*, 85.

25 See Rebecca Hillauer, *Encyclopedia of Arab Women Filmmakers* (Cairo: American Univ in Cairo Press, 2005), 40; and Oliver Leaman, *Companion Encyclopedia of Middle Eastern and North African Film* (London and New York: Routledge, 2001), 30.

26 Talhami, *Palestine in the Egyptian Press*, 233–44

27 See also Dina Jadallah, "Economic Aid to Egypt: Promoting Progress or Subordination?" *Class, Race and Corporate Power* 3, no. 2 (2015): n.p.

28 Avi Shlaim. *The Iron Wall: Israel and the Arab World* (New York: W.W. Norton, 2001), 378.

29 Samih K. Farsoun and Christina Zacharia Hawatmeh, *Palestine and the Palestinians* (Boulder, CO: Westview Press, 1997), 202.

30 Salim Yaqub, *Imperfect Strangers: Americans, Arabs, and U.S.-Middle East Relations in the 1970s* (Ithaca, NY: Cornell University Press, 2016), 270.

31 This tradition of economically boycotting organizations doing business with Israel goes back to the 1948 war, after which the Arab Boycott was formalized, and was soon to be administered by the Damascus-based Arab Boycott Office. See Marwan Iskander, *The Arab Boycott of Israel* (Beirut: Research Center, Palestine Liberation Organization, 1966), 14. Walid Salem places the Arab anti-normalization positions into four categories: "Islam, Arab Marxism, Arab nationalism, and a mix of different ideological groups which all agree on the importance of resisting so-called 'cultural normalization'" (Salem, "The Anti-Normalization Discourse in the Context of Israeli–Palestinian Peace-Building," *Palestine–Israel Journal of Politics, Economics and Culture* 12, no. 1 (2005): 100–109).

32 Antonia Naïm, "'Bab el Chams' ('La Porte du soleil'), un film de Yousry Nasrallah," *La pensée de midi* 14, no. 1 (April 2005): 125.

33 Colla, "Solidarity," 11. See also Mustapha K. El-Sayed, "Egyptian Popular Attitudes toward the Palestinians Since 1977," *Journal of Palestine Studies* 18, no. 4 (1989): 37–51; and Progressive Assembly of National Unionists. "No to the Egyptian–Israeli Treaty." *Middle East Report*, no. 80 (1979): 14–18.

34 Abou-El-Fadl, "The Road to Jerusalem," 9–10. See also Harlow, "Egyptian Intellectuals," 33–58.

35 Naïm, "Bab el Chams," 125.

36 Farsoun and Hawatmeh, *Palestine*, 162.
37 Rashid Khalidi, "The Palestinian Dilemma: PLO Policy after Lebanon," *Journal of Palestine Studies* 15, no. 1 (1985): 90. See also Farsoun and Hawatmeh, *Palestine*, 232.
38 Farsoun and Hawatmeh, *Palestine*, 189.
39 Ibid., 163.
40 Julie Peteet, *Landscape of Hope and Despair: Palestinian Refugee Camps* (University of Pennsylvania Press, 2011) 6–7.
41 Rosemary Sayigh, *Palestinians: From Peasants to Revolutionaries*, New ed. (London; New York: Zed Books, 2007), 115.
42 Peteet, *Landscape*, 6.
43 Ibid., 6.
44 Peteet, *Landscape*, 6–8. For more on the brutal massacre of Palestinian civilians in the Sabra and Shatila refugee camps in September 1982 that was perpetrated by the Phalangists and supported by the Israeli army, see Shlaim, *The Iron Wall*, 428–29.
45 Farsoun and Hawatmeh, *Palestine*, 164.
46 Laleh Khalili, "Heroic and Tragic Pasts: Mnemonic Narratives in the Palestinian Refugee Camps 1," *Critical Sociology* 33, no. 4 (July 2007): 736.
47 Farsoun and Hawatmeh, *Palestine*, 298.
48 Laleh Khalili, "Grass-Roots Commemmorations: Remembering the Land in the Camps of Lebanon," *Journal of Palestine Studies* 34, no. 1 (October 2004): 13.
49 Farsoun and Hawatmeh, *Palestine*, 208.
50 Yezid Sayigh, "Armed Struggle and State Formation," *Journal of Palestine Studies* 26, no. 4 (1997): 30.
51 Farsoun and Hawatmeh, *Palestine*, 266–70.
52 Roy, "De-Development," 64–82.
53 Farsoun and Hawatmeh, *Palestine*, 254.
54 Abou-El-Fadl, "The Road," 10.
55 Naficy, *An Accented Cinema*, 150.
56 Ibid., 105.
57 Elias Khoury, "Rethinking the *Nakba*," *Critical Inquiry* 38, no. 2 (January 2012): 266.
58 Another of Nasrallah's works incidentally carries the title *Ehky Ya Shahrazad* [*Scheherazade, Tell me a Story*] (2009).
59 Open-form aesthetics suit the nostalgic depiction of exilic spaces such as the homeland. Closed-form aesthetics foreground harsher exilic realities, "sites of confinement," as experienced, for instance, in refugee camps. See Naficy, *An Accented Cinema*, 5.
60 "Pourrait-on dire alors que les deux parties sont construites comme la thèse et l'antithèse, la seconde étant comme une mise en question de l'idéologie?" – Y. N.: "Tout à fait." Naïm, "'Bab el Chams'": 124.
61 Lina Khatib, *Filming the Modern Middle East: Politics in the Cinemas of Hollywood and the Arab World* (London: I.B. Tauris, 2006), 150.
62 The term "failure" here refers to the pre-Naksa period. The fact that Kanafani was critiquing the Arab resistance, including the Palestinians, rather than strictly blaming the outsiders/colonizers/Zionists, was perceived as controversial.
63 Zeina Maasri, *Cosmopolitan Radicalism: The Visual Politics of Beirut's Global Sixties* (Cambridge, UK: Cambridge University Press, 2020), 132–33.

64 Nasrallah worked as an editor for *As-Safir* from 1978–1982. Geer, "Yousry Nasrallah," 146. The famous Palestinian cartoonist Naji al-Ali (mentioned in the previous section) also worked for *As-Safir* newspaper in the 1970s.

65 Elias Khoury, "Rethinking," 265–66.

66 Nur Masalha, "Decolonizing Methodology, Reclaiming Memory: Palestinian Oral Histories and Memories of the Nakba," in *An Oral History of the Palestinian Nakba*, eds. Nahla Abdo and Nur Masalha (London: Zed, 2018), 6–39.

67 This schoolroom scene recalls the scene from *The Dupes* in which the eldest of the three Palestinian migrants, Abu Qais, is shown peering into a schoolroom window.

68 Michel Foucault, *Language, Counter-memory, Practice: Selected Essays and Interviews* (Ithaca, NY: Cornell University Press, 1977). Foucault has theorized the notion of "counter-memory" as "an individual's resistance against the official versions of historical continuity." In this concept, memory is critically interrogated, the intent being to understand *who* remembers, the various contexts in which memories are constituted, and also what these memories might oppose.

69 Isabelle Humphries and Laleh Khalili, "Gender of Nakba Memory," in *Nakba: Palestine, 1948, and the Claims of Memory*, eds. Ahmad H. Sa'di and Lila Abu-Lughod (New York: Columbia University Press, 2007), 223.

70 Terri Ginsberg, *Visualizing the Palestinian Struggle: Towards a Critical Analytic of Palestine Solidarity Film* (London: Palgrave Macmillan, 2016), 104.

Conclusion

Almost two decades have passed since *Gate of the Sun* (2004) was produced. These have been politically eventful years, punctuated by the 2011 overthrow of Hosni Mubarak by the Egyptian iteration of a region-wide series of popular uprisings commonly referred to as the Arab Spring, and the subsequent 2013 Egyptian coup, which overthrew the elected President Mohamed Morsi and led to the reconsolidation of a military regime under General Abdelfattah al-Sisi. At the international level, these events followed in the wake of the 2008 financial crisis and accompanying surge in global food prices, which only exacerbated the existing social crisis in Egypt.[1] A preliminary glance at Egyptian politics and culture during this period suggests that its tumultuous events also carried implications for the representation of Palestine in Egyptian cinema.

As noted, starting from the early 1970s, neoliberal reforms, including the privatization of state-owned industries and cuts to social services such as health care and food subsidies, widened the gap between the rich and the poor, and between the state and civil society in Egypt. The factions of commercial and finance capital governing contemporary Egyptian society became increasingly empowered at the expense of "productive, and less mobile, capital," that is, the working class.[2] These domestic developments have been bolstered by growing state repression and surveillance—key contributing factors to the spread and consolidation of neoliberalism in 2000s Egypt—and ongoing U.S. efforts to expand its influence and ensure access for itself and its allies to oil in the region, which has entailed the internationalization of Gulf capital.[3] In the context of Egypt–Palestine relations, these regional and global geopolitical developments serve as a reminder of the "Camp David consensus" that has governed Egypt's foreign policy and role in the Palestinian issue since the 1979 Egypt–Israel peace treaty.[4]

The effects of the contradictions fueled by this neoliberal build-up were felt most acutely by Egyptian workers and young people due to rising unemployment within their ranks, and would gradually bubble to the surface over the course of the 2000s. Along with labor, student, and civil society organizing, popular mobilization for Palestine served as an important incubator for the uprisings that ensued in Egypt in 2011.[5] As previously argued, the ongoing Palestinian struggle had already fostered a broad popular base of international and pan-Arab support that dates back to the earliest stages of organized resistance to Zionist colonization at the beginning of the twentieth century. Yet the Second Palestinian (al-Aqsa) Intifada (2000–2005) would have a decisive, politicizing effect on Egyptians dissatisfied with the bleak social and economic conditions resulting from neoliberalism, inspiring widespread protests in support of Palestine and against the Mubarak administration's persisting alliance with Israel and the United States.[6] Public demonstrations in solidarity with Palestine during the early 2000s marked a critical moment for Egyptians across the political spectrum to realize their shared grievances and demands,[7] providing opportunities for a more consolidated opposition that would converge ideologically around anti-regime, anti-imperialist, and anti-Zionist positions—gesturing toward the necessity of a revived, albeit reconfigured internationalist struggle. According to Maha Abdelrahman (2014),

> An important feature of Egyptian activist networks emerging at that time was their growing links with global networks of activism also struggling to expose the same global power structures, such as militarization of the global system and the economic machinery that supported it.[8]

The Egyptian state initially tolerated and sought to identify itself with the pro-Palestine protests in an attempt to prevent its own decreasing legitimacy, but the tables would soon turn when the state itself became the protesters' main target in 2011.[9] Post-2011 Egypt has seen no significant structural transformation or foreign policy change with respect to Palestine/Israel despite optimism at the beginning of the ultimately short-lived Morsi administration. Under Sisi's military regime, economic and regional "stability" as well as national "security" have become stated priorities, whereupon Palestinian liberation has been marginalized within the official discourse.[10] The Egyptian normalization of Zionism has also played out through the expansion of so-called QIZs (Qualifying Industrial Zones), an

Egyptian-Israeli economic cooperation project initiated in the early 2000s to allow goods produced in Egypt to access U.S. and Israeli markets without restriction.

These political and economic developments also entailed considerable ramifications for cinema, as the first published works on the subject, such as Ahmed Ghazal's *Egyptian Cinema and the 2011 Revolution: Film Production and Representing Dissent* (2020), have proposed. Ghazal observes that, since the late 1990s, an "oligopoly" of production and distribution companies has exerted increasing influence over the Egyptian film industry,[11] where commercial genre films (comedies, romantic dramas and action films) are therefore maintaining dominance.[12] Recalling the discussion of revolutionary melodramas in Chapter One, we find that here, too, such trivial and ostensibly apolitical entertainment films may still contain the seeds of dissent.[13] Hence, a critical reading of recent Egyptian film productions is likely also to reference contemporary social contradictions and exacerbated political repression among the wider populace, not least in terms of its abiding solidarity with Palestine.

Such sociopolitical contradictions are in fact commonly negotiated through media. In Egyptian commercial cinema of the early 2000s, several films lent expression to popular discontent with Egyptian normalization efforts. These include the comedy, *Al-Sifara fi-l-ʿImara* [*The Embassy in the Building*] (Amr Arafa, 2005), and the spy thriller, *Wlad al-ʿAmm* [The Cousins] (Sherif Arafa, 2009). Scholars have argued that these films, produced during a period of legitimation crisis for the Mubarak administration, symptomatized a moment of calculated political tolerance and "decompression" following the events of September 11, 2001, designed to provide safety valves for absorbing and mediating rising sociopolitical tensions.[14] These popular films certainly did appear to reject Egyptian rapprochement with Israel, yet their patriotic undertones also subverted their critiques of Zionism.[15]

Alongside these mainstream tendencies, technological developments such as the rise of social media would facilitate new modes of self-expression and inspire "more independent projects."[16] The plethora of alternative, lower-budget films produced in the two decades preceding the 2011 uprisings anticipated them through critical cinematography and thematic attention to social discontent.[17] Future scholarship might well investigate the impact of Israeli normalization on Egyptian cinema of this period or consider the figuration of Palestine—implicit, allegorical—in these politically charged, pre-revolution, largely Egypt-centered films.

Although the Arab uprisings were heralded as an occasion for harnessing visual technology in new ways, for example uploading images and sharing information on social media platforms, most of these were commercial, such as Facebook and

Twitter, while post-2011 Egyptian media have become heavily monitored and increasingly monopolized by production companies such as Synergy, which is owned by the state-supported conglomerate, Egyptian Media Group.[18] A production that typifies the current administration's relationship with the media industry is the blockbuster war film *Al-Mamar* [*The Passage*] (2019), the most expensive Egyptian film to date.[19] This lavish, labor-intensive production represents Palestine only tangentially while propping up a centered image of the Egyptian state. Its focus on the protracted interval between the Six-Day War and the October War works ideologically to challenge common understandings of the Defeat in a revisionist direction that in fact underwrites the contemporary, *anti*-Palestinian militarism that is part and parcel of Israeli normalization.

Emerging scholarship on post-revolutionary Egyptian cinema has taken steps toward interrogating the extent to which it may have changed in response to the Arab uprisings and their aftermath.[20] An ostensibly more independent filmmaking wave, "New Egyptian Cinema," has been theorized in view of an evident alteration in production style and cinematic language.[21] This cinema, as Amir Taha describes it in *Film and Counterculture in the 2011 Egyptian Uprising* (2021),

> is marked by small and independent funding that varies from private funding, international grants to independent cooperatives, different subject matters than those presented in the commercial mainstream cinema in Egypt, and a new filmic language which develops new modes of production and new aesthetics in the context of Egyptian cinema.[22]

In fact, blockbusters like *The Passage* are not typical of recent Egyptian cinema, for which low-budget films have been predominant since 2011.[23] Critics of this tendency claim that the newer films lack "truly independent" characteristics such as "counter-voices, counter-techniques, and counter-arguments to hegemonic cinematic systems and discourse."[24] Representation of the Palestinian struggle, among other underrepresented social issues, has indeed been limited.[25] It is of course arguable that such limitation is at least partly attributable to the minimal structural change in Egypt after 2011, which, along with the draconian measures taken by the Sisi regime to enforce an exceedingly oppressive and exploitative status quo, has hindered the formation of a genuine "post-revolution film movement."[26]

This book has sought to theorize the changing political dynamics underpinning Egyptian cinema's historical engagement with Palestine across three paradigmatic moments. By integrating textual analysis with politico-historical contextualization, my aim has been to ascertain how the representation of Palestine in Egyptian cinema has altered in conjunction with shifting local, regional, and international conditions throughout the second half of the twentieth century and into the new millennium. Analyzing these dynamics has often entailed pushing the boundaries of the nation-state and, with them, the scholarly framing of "national cinemas." My research shows that when we encounter the question of Palestine in cinema, diasporic conditions, and solidarity culture, we must confront the (im)mobility bound up with (trans)national reality. Acknowledging the historical presence of Palestine in Egyptian cinema, in other words, compels us to deconstruct the traditional notion of the nation-state as primary determinant of meaning, and instead read the relationship between politics and aesthetics both within and against the shifting flows of transnational capital.

In its effort to critique hegemonic representations of Palestine in Egyptian industry cinema while highlighting pan/transnational challenges to them, *Representations of Palestine in Egyptian Cinema* intervenes into a growing body of scholarship on Arab and transnational film studies. But where do we go from here? In a 1973 interview, the late Palestinian revolutionary filmmaker, Mostafa Abu Ali (1938–2001), offered his thoughts on the representation of Palestine in Arab cinema. In his view, it is important to make the distinction between two categories: films made by the private sector for commercial ends, and films produced by the public sector that are typically compatible with the state's official posturing. He describes the former category as "abhorrent" for having produced films that exploit and commodify the legitimate sense of solidarity shared among Arab peoples with the Palestinian cause. He describes the latter category, which has produced far fewer films, as less condemnable despite its pervasive tendency to privilege the concerns of the producing countries over those of the resistance.[27] *Representations of Palestine in Egyptian Cinema* has worked to elucidate a similar point, offering a critical reconsideration of an important but largely neglected body of Egyptian films in terms of their representation of Palestine under, respectively, private, state-endorsed, and alternative production conditions.

An oft-misrepresented subject, the Palestinian struggle has nonetheless consistently fostered the creation of radical film aesthetics. This book's critical metanarrative on the ideologically contested and politically charged question of Palestinian "representation" through the mediating prism of shifting pan/transnationalisms from the perspective of Egyptian cinema hopes to solidify that creative direction. As Edward Said summarizes in his preface to *Dreams of a Nation* (2006), the question of Palestine and its representation must always be understood as part of a political struggle over "the dialectic of the visible and the invisible."[28] Recognizing Palestine at the (in)visible nexus of a critical selection of Egyptian films, this book celebrates the enduring importance of Palestine to the Egyptian popular and cinematic imaginary.

Notes

1 Adam Hanieh, *Lineages of Revolt: Issues of Contemporary Capitalism in the Middle East* (Chicago: Haymarket, 2013), 146.
2 Sean F. McMahon, *Crisis and Class War in Egypt: Social Reproduction, Factional Realignments and the Global Political Economy* (London: Zed, 2016), 164.
3 See also Sara Salem, *Anticolonial Afterlives in Egypt: The Politics of Hegemony* (Cambridge, UK: Cambridge University Press, 2020), 229–30. Besides strengthening economic linkages with the Gulf states (especially Qatar and Saudi Arabia), the United States has also continued to exert influence over Egyptian politics, for instance by periodically supporting the Muslim Brotherhood. See Ibrahim G Aoudé, "Egypt: Revolutionary Process and Global Capitalist Crisis," *Arab Studies Quarterly* 35, no. 3 (2013): 248.
4 Ewan Stein, *Representing Israel in Modern Egypt: Ideas, Intellectuals and Foreign Policy from Nasser to Mubarak* (London: Bloomsbury Academic, 2012), 173–74.
5 Reem Abou-El-Fadl, "The Road to Jerusalem through Tahrir Square: Anti-Zionism and Palestine in the 2011 Egyptian Revolution," *Journal of Palestine Studies* 41, no. 2 (January 2012): 11–12.
6 Hanieh, *Lineages*, 163.
7 Rabab El-Mahdi, "The Democracy Movement: Cycles of Protest," in *Egypt: The Moment of Change*, eds. Rabab El-Mahdi and Philip Marfleet (London and New York: Zed, 2009), 94. As El-Mahdi describes, the grassroots Egyptian Movement for Change, Kefaya ("enough"), for example, originated in the activist networks that were formed during the Intifada. Kefaya called for democracy and was able to overcome ideological differences and rival oppositional forces and translate popular solidarity with Palestinians into mass campaigns.
8 Maha M. Abdelrahman, *Egypt's Long Revolution: Protest Movements and Uprisings* (Abingdon and New York: Routledge, 2015), 33.
9 Ibid., 32, 59.
10 Khaled Elgindy, "Egypt, Israel, Palestine," *The Cairo Review of Global Affairs* 6 (Summer 2012): 177.
11 Ahmed Ghazal, *Egyptian Cinema and the 2011 Revolution: Film Production and Representing Dissent* (London: Bloomsbury Academic, 2022), 43.
12 Ibid., 43, 67–9.
13 Ibid., 69.
14 Ibid., 333, 342.
15 Spy films and comedies ridiculing Israelis proliferated between the 1980s and early 2000s. In them, Egypt–Israel relations tend to be represented through depictions of Egypt prevailing over Israel in war, mainly through references to the October War.
Mouline, "Dégage'," 342.
16 Ghazal, *Egyptian Cinema*, 9.
17 Following films such as *Al-Irhab wal Kabab* [*Terrorism and Kebab*] (Sherif Arafa, 1992), which was one of the first of its kind to illustrate the pre-2011 sociopolitical and economic conditions in Egypt, exemplary films of this period, according to Mohammed Tabishat, include *Eish arit morour* [*Traffic Light*] (Khairy Bishara, 1995), *Muwatin wa Mukhbir wa Harami* [*A Citizen, a Detective and a Thief*] (Daoud Abdel Sayed, 2001), *'Imarat Ya'qubiyan* [*The Yacoubian Building*] (Marwan Hamed, 2006), *Heyaa Fawda* [This Is Chaos] (Youssef Chahine, 2007), and *Genenet al-Asmak*

[*The Aquarium*] (Yousry Nasrallah, 2008). Tabishat, "Society in Cinema: Anticipating the Revolution in Egyptian Fiction and Movies," *Social Research* 79, no. 2 (2012): 378.

18 Synergy is owned by the head of the intelligence-affiliated Egyptian Media Group (EMG). It is the newest step in the state's ongoing bid to monopolize all forms of media and artistic production in Egypt. See Mohamed al-Aswany, "An Industry under Threat: Ramadan 2019, Brought to You by Egyptian Media Group," trans. Mariam Ibrahim, *Mada Masr* 23 December 2018, https://www.madamasr.com/en/2018/12/23/feature/culture/an-industry-under-threat-ramadan-2019-brought-to-you-by-egyptian-media-group/.

19 Joseph Fahim, "Egypt's Biggest Film: How The Passage Owes a Debt to Sisi," *Middle East Eye* 21 June 2019, http://www.middleeasteye.net/discover/egypt-film-mamar-arab-israeli-1967-war-assad-ezz.

20 See Alisa Lebow, "Seeing Revolution Non-Linearly: https://filmingrevolution.org/" *Visual Anthropology* 29, no. 3 (May 2016): 278–95.

21 Amir Taha, *Film and Counterculture in the 2011 Egyptian Uprising* (Cham, Switzerland: Palgrave Macmillan, 2021). The book examines five recent Egyptian films: Ahmed Abdallah's *Microphone* (2010), his *Farsh wa Ghatta* [*Rags and Tatters*] (2013), Hala Lotfy's *Al-Khoroug Lel-Nahar* [*Coming Forth by Day*] (2013), Tamer El Said's *Akher Ayam El Madina* [*In the Last Days of the City*] (2016), and Mohamed Diab's *Eshtebak* [*Clash*] (2016).

22 Taha, *Film and Counterculture*, 10.

23 Ghazal, *Egyptian Cinema*, 7.

24 Samirah Alkassim, "Indie Blues: Alternative Cairo?" *Bidoun* 11 (Summer 2007), https://bidoun.org/articles/indie-blues.

25 Nadim Jarjoura, "The Current State of Arab Cinema: The Stories of Individuals … and an Update on Documentary Films," *Contemporary Arab Affairs* 7, no. 2 (April 2014): 222.

26 Ghazal, *Egyptian Cinema*, 9.

27 See "Entretien Avec Muçtapha Abu Ali et Hassan Abu Ghanima: 'Nous voulons un cinema populaire dans lequel le people se retrouve en train de construire l'Histoire,'" in Guy Hennebelle and Khemaïs Khayati, *La Palestine et le cinéma* (Paris: Éditions du Centenaire, 1977), 38–44.

28 Edward Said, "Preface," in *Dreams of a Nation: On Palestinian Cinema*, ed. Hamid Dabashi (London and New York: Verso, 2006), 1.

Filmography

Akher Ayam El Madina [*In the Last Days of the City*] (Tamer El Said, Egypt/Germany/UK/UAE, 2016).
Al-'Asfour [*The Sparrow*] (Youssef Chahine, Egypt, 1972).
Al-Azima [*Determination*] (Kamal Selim, Egypt, 1939).
Al-Bab al-Maftouh [*The Open Door*] (Henry Barakat, Egypt, 1963).
Al-Fahd [*The Leopard*] (Nabil Maleh, Syria, 1972).
Al-Irhab wal Kabab [*Terrorism and Kebab*] (Sherif Arafa, Egypt, 1992).
Al-Khoroug Lel-Nahar [*Coming Forth by Day*] (Hala Lotfy, Egypt, 2013).
Al-Makhdu'un [*The Dupes*] (Tawfik Saleh, Syria, 1972).
Al-Mamar [*The Passage*] (Sherif Arafa, Egypt, 2019).
Al-Nasser Salah Ad-Din [*Saladin the Victorious*] (Youssef Chahine, Egypt, 1963).
Al-Sifara fi-l-'Imara [*The Embassy in the Building*] (Amr Arafa, Egypt, 2005).
Al-Sikkin [*The Knife*] (Khaled Hamadeh, Syria, 1972).
Al-Zilal fi al-Ganib al-Akhar [*Shadows on the Other Side*] (Ghaleb Chaath, Palestine, 1973).
Allah Ma'ana [*God Is with Us*] (Ahmad Badrakhan, Egypt, 1955).
Antar bin Shaddad [*Antar the Black Prince*] (Niazi Mostafa, Egypt, 1961).
Ard al-Abtal [*Land of Heroes*] (Niazi Mostafa, Egypt, 1953).
Ard al-Salam [*Land of Peace*] (Kamal el-Sheikh, Egypt, 1957).
Ayam al-Sadat [*Days of Sadat*] (Mohamed Khan, Egypt, 2001).
Ba'idan 'an al-Watan [*Far from the Homeland*] (Qais al-Zubaidi, Syria, 1969).
Bab al-Shams [*Gate of the Sun*] (Yousry Nasrallah, Egypt/France, 2004).

Darb al-Mahabil [*Alley of Fools*] (Tawfik Saleh, Egypt, 1955).
Eish arit morour [*Traffic Light*] (Khairy Bishara, Egypt, 1995).
Ehky Ya Shahazad [*Scheherazade, Tell Me a Story*] (Yousry Nasrallah, Egypt, 2009).
Eshtebak [*Clash*] (Mohamed Diab, Egypt/France/Germany, 2016).
Farsh wa Ghatta [*Rags and Tatters*] (Ahmed Abdallah, Egypt, 2013).
Fatat min Falastin [*A Girl from Palestine*] (Mahmoud Zulficar, Egypt, 1948).
Genenet al-Asmak [*The Aquarium*] (Yousry Nasrallah, Egypt, 2008).
Heyaa Fawda [*This Is Chaos*] (Youssef Chahine/Khaled Youssef, Egypt, 2007).
'Imarat Ya'qubiyan [*The Yacoubian Building*] (Marwan Hamed, Egypt, 2006).
Kafr Kassem (Borhane Alaouié, Syria, 1974).
Microphone (Ahmed Abdallah, Egypt, 2010).
Muwatin wa Mukhbir wa Harami [*A Citizen, a Detective and a Thief*] (Daoud Abdel Sayed, Egypt, 2001).
Nadia (Fatin Abdel Wahab, Egypt, 1949).
Nagi El-Ali (Atef El Tayeb, Egypt, 1991).
Nasser 56 (Mohamed Fadel, Egypt, 1996).
Rijal taht al-Shams [*Men Under the Sun*] (Marwan Mu'azzin/Muhammad Shahin/Nabil Maleh, Syria, 1970).
Sa'iq al-Shahinah [*The Truck Driver*] (Boško Vučinić, Syria, 1966).
Sawwaq al-Utubis [*The Bus Driver*] (Atef El Tayeb, Egypt, 1982).
Shahadat al-Filastinyyin fi Zaman al-Harb [*Testimonies of Palestinians in the Time of War*] (Qais al-Zubaidi, Syria, 1972).
Ughniyya 'ala al-Mamar [*A Song on the Passage*] (Ali Abd El-Khalek, Egypt, 1972).
Wlad al-'Amm [*The Cousins*] (Sherif Arafa, Egypt, 2009).
Yawmiyat Na'ib fi al-Aryaf [*Diary of a Country Prosecutor*] (Tawfik Saleh, Egypt, 1969).
Yom Murr, Yom Helw [*Bitter Day, Sweet Day*] (Khairy Bishara, Egypt, 1988).
Zaugat Ragul Muhim [*Wife of an Important Man*] (Mohamed Khan, Egypt, 1987).

Bibliography

Abadi, Jacob. "Egypt's Policy towards Israel: The Impact of Foreign and Domestic Constraints." *Israel Affairs* 12, no. 1 (January 2006): 159–76.

Abdallah, Ahmed. *The Student Movement and National Politics in Egypt, 1923–1973*. London: Al Saqi, 1985.

Abdel-Malek, Anouar. "Nasserism And Socialism." *Socialist Register* 1 (March 1964): 38–55.

Abdel-Malek, Anouar. *Egypt: Military Society: The Army Regime, the Left, and Social Change Under Nasser*, trans. Charles Lam Markmann. New York: Random House, 1968.

Abdelrahman, Maha M. *Egypt's Long Revolution: Protest Movements and Uprisings*. Abingdon and New York: Routledge, 2015.

Abou-El-Fadl, Reem. "The Road to Jerusalem through Tahrir Square: Anti-Zionism and Palestine in the 2011 Egyptian Revolution." *Journal of Palestine Studies* 41, no. 2 (January 2012): 6–26.

Abou-El-Fadl, Reem. *Foreign Policy as Nation Making: Turkey and Egypt in the Cold War*. Cambridge, UK: Cambridge University Press, 2018.

Abraham, Sameer. "The PLO at the Crossroads: Moderation, Encirclement, Future Prospects." *MERIP Reports*, no. 80 (1979): 5–26.

Ahmed, Leila. *A Border Passage: From Cairo to America--A Woman's Journey*. New York: Penguin, 2012.

Al-Aswany, Mohamed. "An Industry under Threat: Ramadan 2019, Brought to You by Egyptian Media Group," trans. Mariam Ibrahim, *Mada Masr*, 23 December 2018, https://www.madamasr.com/en/2018/12/23/feature/culture/an-industry-under-threat-ramadan-2019-brought-to-you-by-egyptian-media-group/. Access date: 12 April 2023

Al-Azm, Sadik. *Self-Criticism after the Defeat*. London: Al Saqi, 2012.

Alexander, Livia. "Foreword," in *Insights into Syrian Cinema: Essays and Conversations with Contemporary Filmmakers*, ed. Rasha Salti, 21– 44. New York: Rattapallax, 2006.

Alkassim, Samirah. "Indie Blues: Alternative Cairo?" *Bidoun* 11 (Summer 2007), https://bidoun.org/articles/indie-blues.

Alkassim, Samirah and Nezar Andary. *The Cinema of Muhammad Malas*. Cham, Switzerland: Palgrave Macmillan, 2018.

Amin, Samir. "A Note on the Concept of Delinking." *Review (Fernand Braudel Center)* 10, no. 3 (1987): 435–44.

Amin, Samir. *The People's Spring: The Future of the Arab Revolution*. Nairobi: Pambuzuka Press, 2012.

Anderson, Benedict. *Imagined Communities: Reflections on the Origin and Spread of Nationalism*. London and New York: Verso, 1991.

Antonius, Soraya. "The Palestine Cause in the Cinema," *Journal of Palestine Studies* 7, no. 2 (January 1978): 120–5.

Aoudé, Ibrahim G. "Egypt: Revolutionary Process and Global Capitalist Crisis." *Arab Studies Quarterly* 35, no. 3 (2013): 241–54.

Armbrust, Walter. *Mass Mediations: New Approaches to Popular Culture in the Middle East and Beyond*. Berkeley and Los Angeles: University of California Press, 2000.

Armbrust, Walter. "Egyptian Cinema On Stage and Off," in *Off Stage/On Display: Intimacy and Ethnography in the Age of Public Culture*, ed. Andrew Shryock, 69–100. Stanford, CA: Stanford University Press, 2004.

Armbrust, Walter. "Audiovisual Media and History of the Arab Middle East," in *Middle East Historiographies: Narrating the Twentieth Century*, eds. I. Gershoni, Amy Singer, and Y. Hakan Erdem, 288–313. Seattle: University of Washington Press, 2006.

Ashour, Amro "Filastin fi al-aflam al-masriyya mundhu 1948 hatta bab el-shams." *Magallat romman al-thaqafiyah*. https://rommanmag.com/view/posts/postDetails?id=4407.

Ashour, Radwa. *The Woman from Tantoura: A Palestinian Novel*. Oxford, UK: Oxford University Press, 2014.

Badran, Margot. *Feminists, Islam, and Nation: Gender and the Making of Modern Egypt*. Princeton, NJ: Princeton University Press, 1995.

Baker, Raymond William. *Egypt's Uncertain Revolution under Nasser and Sadat*. Cambridge, MA: Harvard University Press, 1978.

Beinin, Joel. "The Communist Movement and Nationalist Political Discourse in Nasirist Egypt." *Middle East Journal* 41, no. 4 (1987): 568–84.

Bier, Laura. *Revolutionary Womanhood: Feminisms, Modernity, and the State in Nasser's Egypt*. Stanford, CA: Stanford University Press, 2011.

Bouzid, Nouri, "New Realism in Arab Cinema: The Defeat-Conscious Cinema." *Alif: Journal of Comparative Poetics*, no. 15 (1995): 242–50.

Brittain, Victoria. *Love and Resistance in the Films of Mai Masri*. Cham, Switzerland: Palgrave Macmillan, 2021.

Burris, Greg. *The Palestinian Idea: Film, Media, and the Radical Imagination*. Philadelphia: Temple University Press, 2019.

Colla, Elliott. "Solidarity in the Time of Anti-Normalization." *Middle East Report*, no. 224 (2002): 10–15.

Collins, John Martin. *Global Palestine*. London: Hurst, 2011.

Cordon, Joel. "Class-Crossed Lovers: Popular Film and Social Change in Nasser's New Egypt." *Quarterly Review of Film and Video* 18, no. 4 (October 2001): 385–96.

Dabashi, Hamid, ed. *Dreams of a Nation: On Palestinian Cinema*. London and New York: Verso, 2006.

Davis, Rochelle. *Palestinian Village Histories: Geographies of the Displaced*. Stanford, CA: Stanford University Press, 2010.

Denes, Nick. "Between Form and Function." *Middle East Journal of Culture and Communication* 7, no. 2 (2014): 219–41.

Dickinson, Kay. *Arab Film and Video Manifestos: Forty-Five Years of the Moving Image Amid Revolution*. Cham: Springer International Publishing, 2018.

Dickinson, Kay. *Arab Cinema Travels: Transnational Syria, Palestine, Dubai and Beyond*. London: British Film Institute, 2016.

Dickinson, Kay. "The State of Labor and Labor for the State: Syrian and Egyptian Cinema beyond the 2011 Uprisings." *Framework: The Journal of Cinema and Media* 53, no. 1 (2012): 99–116.

Dickinson, Kay. "'I Have One Daughter and That Is Egyptian Cinema': `Azīza Amīr amid the Histories and Geographies of National Allegory." *Camera Obscura: Feminism, Culture, and Media Studies* 22, no. 1 (2007): 137–77.

Doane, Mary Ann. *The Desire to Desire: The Woman's Film of the 1940s*. 9. [Dr.]. Bloomington: Indiana University Press, 1999.

Doran, Michael Scott. *Pan-Arabism Before Nasser: Egyptian Power Politics and the Palestine Question*. Oxford, UK: University Press, 1999.

El-Abed, Oroub. *Unprotected: Palestinians in Egypt since 1948*. Washington, ON: Institute for Palestine Studies / International Development Research Centre, 2009.

Elgindy, Khaled. "Egypt, Israel, Palestine." *The Cairo Review of Global Affairs* 6 (Summer 2012): 170–81.

El-Mahdi, Rabab. "The Democracy Movement: Cycles of Protest," in *Egypt: The Moment of Change*, eds. Rabab El-Mahdi and Philip Marfleet, 87–102. London and New York: Zed, 2009.

Elsaesser, Thomas. "Tales of Sound and Fury: Observations on the Family Melodrama," in *Imitations of Life*, ed. Marcia Landy, 68–92. Detroit: Wayne State University Press.

El-Sayed, Mustapha K. "Egyptian Popular Attitudes toward the Palestinians Since 1977." *Journal of Palestine Studies* 18, no. 4 (1989): 37–51.

El-Shammaa, Magdy Mounir. *The National Imaginarium: A History of Egyptian Filmmaking.* Cairo: American University in Cairo Press, 2021.

Ende, Werner. "The Palestine Conflict as Reflected in Contemporary Arabic Literature," in *The Contemporary Middle Eastern Scene: Basic Issues and Major Trends*, eds. Gustav Stein and Udo Steinbach, 154–67. Opladen: Leske und Budrich, 1979.

Erakat, Noura. *Justice for Some: Law and the Question of Palestine.* Stanford, CA: Stanford University Press, 2020.

Fahim, Joseph. "Egypt's Biggest Film: How the Passage Owes a Debt to Sisi," *Middle East Eye* 21 June 2019, http://www.middleeasteye.net/discover/egypt-film-mamar-arab-israeli-1967-war-assad-ezz.

Fahmy, Ziad. *Ordinary Egyptians: Creating the Modern Nation through Popular Culture.* Stanford, CA: Stanford University Press, 2011.

Farid Samir, *Madkhal ila tarikh al-sinima al-'arabiya.* Cairo: Egyptian General Book Institute, 2001.

Farsoun, Samih K., and Christina Zacharia Hawatmeh. *Palestine and the Palestinians.* Boulder, CO: Westview Press, 1997.

Foucault, Michel. *Language, Counter-memory, Practice: Selected Essays and Interviews.* Ithaca, NY: Cornell University Press, 1977.

Fouzi El-Asmar, "Continuing the Palestinian Struggle, Part 2," interview by Terri Ginsberg, *ZNet* 8 October 2021, https://www.academia.edu/2029583/Continuing_the_Palestinian_Struggle_Part_2.

Gaffney, Jane. "The Egyptian Cinema: Industry and Art in a Changing Society." *Arab Studies Quarterly* 9, no. 1 (1987): 53–75.

Geer, Benjamin Geer. "Yousry Nasrallah: The Pursuit of Autonomy in the Arab and European Film Markets (Egypt)," in *Ten Arab Filmmakers: Political Dissent and Social Critique*, ed. Josef Gugler, 142–64. Bloomington: Indiana University Press, 2015.

Gerges, Fawaz A. "Egypt and the 1948 War: Internal Conflict and Regional Ambition," in *The War for Palestine: Rewriting the History of 1948*, eds. Eugene L. Rogan and Avi Shlaim, 2nd ed., 151–77. Cambridge, UK: Cambridge University Press, 2007.

Gerges, Fawaz A. *Making the Arab World: Nasser, Qutb, and the Clash That Shaped the Middle East.* Princeton, NJ: Princeton University Press, 2018.

Gershoni, Israel. "The Muslim Brothers and the Arab Revolt in Palestine, 1936–39." *Middle Eastern Studies* 22, no. 3 (1986): 367–97.

Gertz, Nurith, and George Khleifi. *Palestinian Cinema: Landscape, Trauma and Memory.* Edinburgh: Edinburgh University Press, 2008.

Ghazal, Ahmed. *Egyptian Cinema and the 2011 Revolution: Film Production and Representing Dissent.* London: Bloomsbury Academic, 2022.

Ginsberg, Terri. *Visualizing the Palestinian Struggle: Towards a Critical Analytic of Palestine Solidarity Film.* London: Palgrave Macmillan, 2016.

Ginsberg, Terri. *Films of Arab Loutfi and Heiny Srour: Studies in Palestine Solidarity Cinema.* Cham, Switzerland: Palgrave Macmillan, 2021.

Ginsberg, Terri, and Chris Lippard. *Historical Dictionary of Middle Eastern Cinema.* 2nd ed. Lanham, MD: Rowman and Littlefield, 2020.

Ginsberg, Terri, and Chris Lippard. *Cinema of the Arab World: Contemporary Directions in Theory and Practice.* Cham: Springer International Publishing, 2020.

Gledhill, Christine. "Christine Gledhill on 'Stella Dallas' and Feminist Film Theory." *Cinema Journal* 25, no. 4 (1986): 44–8.

Gordon, Joel S. *Nasser's Blessed Movement: Egypt's Free Officers and the July Revolution.* New York: Oxford University Press, 1992.

Gordon, Joel S. *Revolutionary Melodrama: Popular Film and Civic Identity in Nasser's Egypt.* Chicago: Middle East Documentation Center, 2002.

Habashneh, Khadijah. *Fursan Al-Sinima: Sira Wahdat Aflam Filastin.* Amman: Al-Ahlia lil-Nashr wal-Tawzi', 2019.

Haddad, Toufic. *Palestine Ltd.: Neoliberalism and Nationalism in the Occupied Territory.* London: I.B. Tauris, 2016.

Haddad, William W. *The Arab–Israeli Conflict in the Arab Press: The First Three Decades.* London: Intellect, 2018.

Hamam, Iman. "Exceptions to the Rule: The Mechanics of War and the Institution in Egyptian Cinema," in *Cinema of the Arab World: Contemporary Directions in Theory and Practice*, eds. Terri Ginsberg and Chris Lippard, 352–53. Cham, Switzerland: Palgrave Macmillan, 2020.

Hanieh, Adam. *Lineages of Revolt: Issues of Contemporary Capitalism in the Middle East.* Chicago, Illinois: Haymarket, 2013.

Harlow, Barbara. "History and Endings: Ghassan Kanafani's Men in the Sun and Tawfiq Salih's *The Duped.*" *Minnesota Review* 25, no. 1 (1985): 102–13.

Harlow, Barbara. "Egyptian Intellectuals and the Debate on the 'Normalization of Cultural Relations.'" *Cultural Critique* no. 4 (1986): 33–55.

Harrison, Olivia C. *Transcolonial Maghreb: Imagining Palestine in the Era of Decolonization.* Stanford, CA: Stanford University Press, 2015.

Hennebelle, Guy, and Khemaïs Khayati. *La Palestine et le cinéma.* Paris: Éditions du Centenaire, 1977.

Higbee, Will. *Post-Beur Cinema: North African Emigre and Maghrebi-French Filmmaking in France since 2000.* Edinburgh: Edinburgh University Press, 2013.

Hillauer, Rebecca. *Encyclopedia of Arab Women Filmmakers.* Cairo: American University in Cairo Press, 2005.

Humphries, Isabelle, and Laleh Khalili, "Gender of Nakba Memory," in *Nakba: Palestine, 1948, and the Claims of Memory*, eds. Ahmad H. Sa'di and Lila Abu-Lughod, 207–28. New York: Columbia University Press, 2007.

Hussein, Mahmoud. *Class Conflict in Egypt: 1945–1970.* New York and London: Monthly Review Press, 1973.

Ibrahim, Bashar. *Filastin Fi Al-Sinima al-'Arabiyyah*. Damascus: Wezarat al-Thaqafah, 2005.

Iskander, Marwan. *The Arab Boycott of Israel*. Beirut: Research Center, Palestine Liberation Organization, 1966.

Ismael, Tareq Y. *The Arab Left. Contemporary Issues in the Middle East Series 4*. Syracuse, NY: Syracuse University Press, 1976.

Ismael, Tareq Y. *The Communist Movement in the Arab World*. London and New York: Routledge Curzon, 2005.

Ismael, Tareq Y., and Rifa'at El-Sa'id. *The Communist Movement in Egypt, 1920–1988*. Syracuse, NY: Syracuse University Press, 1990.

Jadallah, Dina. "Economic Aid to Egypt: Promoting Progress or Subordination?" *Class, Race and Corporate Power* 3, no. 2 (2015): n.p.

Jameson, Fredric. *The Political Unconscious: Narrative as a Socially Symbolic Act*. Ithaca, NY: Cornell University Press, 1981.

Jameson, Fredric. "Third-World Literature in the Era of Multinational Capitalism," *Social Text* 15 (1986): 65–88.

Jameson, Fredric. "Cognitive Mapping," in *Marxism and the Interpretation of Culture*, eds. Cary Nelson and Lawrence Grossberg, 347–60. Urbana-Champaign and Chicago: University of Illinois Press, 1988.

Jankowski, James P. *Nasser's Egypt, Arab Nationalism, and the United Arab Republic*. Boulder, CO: Lynne Rienner, 2002.

Jarjoura, Nadim. "The Current State of Arab Cinema: The Stories of Individuals ... and an Update on Documentary Films." *Contemporary Arab Affairs* 7, no. 2 (April 2014): 209–24.

Joseph, Sabrina. "Representations of Private/Public Domains: The Feminine Ideal and Modernist Agendas in Egyptian Film, Mid–1950s–1980s." *Frontiers: A Journal of Women Studies* 30, no. 2 (2009): 72–109.

Kadri, Ali. *The Unmaking of Arab Socialism*. New York: Anthem Press, 2016.

Kandil, Hazem. *Soldiers, Spies, and Statesmen: Egypt's Road to Revolt*. London and New York: Verso, 2014.

Karmi, Ghada. *Married to Another Man: Israel's Dilemma in Palestine*. London: Pluto Press, 2015.

Khalili, Laleh. "Grass-Roots Commemorations: Remembering the Land in the Camps of Lebanon." *Journal of Palestine Studies* 34, no. 1 (October 2004): 6–22.

Khalili, Laleh. "Heroic and Tragic Pasts: Mnemonic Narratives in the Palestinian Refugee Camps 1." *Critical Sociology* 33, no. 4 (July 2007): 731–59.

Khatib, Lina. *Filming the Modern Middle East: Politics in the Cinemas of Hollywood and the Arab World*. London: I.B. Tauris, 2006.

Khouri, Malek. *The Arab National Project in Youssef Chahine's Cinema*. Cairo: American University in Cairo Press, 2010.

Khoury, Elias. "Rethinking the *Nakba*." *Critical Inquiry* 38, no. 2 (January 2012): 250–66.

Leaman, Oliver. *Companion Encyclopedia of Middle Eastern and North African Film*. London and New York: Routledge, 2001.

Lebow, Alisa. "Seeing Revolution Non-Linearly: www.Filmingrevolution.Org." *Visual Anthropology* 29, no. 3 (May 2016): 278–95.

Lesch, Ann Mosely, and Mark A. Tessler. *Israel, Egypt, and the Palestinians: From Camp David to Intifada*. Indianapolis: Indiana University Press, 1989.

Maasri, Zeina. *Cosmopolitan Radicalism: The Visual Politics of Beirut's Global Sixties*. Cambridge, UK: Cambridge University Press, 2020.

Maatouk, Tamara. "Understanding the Public Sector in Egyptian Cinema: A State Venture." *Cairo Papers in Social Science* 35, no. 3 (2019): 1–87.

Masalha, Nur. *The Politics of Denial: Israel and the Palestinian Refugee Problem*. London: Pluto Press, 2003.

Masalha, Nur. "Decolonizing Methodology, Reclaiming Memory: Palestinian Oral Histories and Memories of the Nakba," in *An Oral History of the Palestinian Nakba*, eds. Nahla Abdo and Nur Masalha, 6–39. London: Zed, 2018.

Massad, Joseph. "Liberating Songs: Palestine Put to Music." *Journal of Palestine Studies* 32, no. 3 (April 2003): 21–38.

Massad, Joseph. "The Weapon of Culture: Cinema in the Palestinian Liberation Struggle." In *Dreams of a Nation: On Palestinian Cinema*, ed. Hamid Dabashi, 32–44. London: Verso, 2006.

Mayer, Thomas. "Egypt's 1948 Invasion of Palestine." *Middle Eastern Studies* 22, no. 1 (1986): 20–36.

Mehrez, Samia. *Egyptian Writers Between History and Fiction: Essays on Naguib Mahfouz, Sonallah Ibrahim, and Gamal Al-Ghitani*. Cairo: American University in Cairo Press, 1994.

McMahon, Sean F. *Crisis and Class War in Egypt: Social Reproduction, Factional Realignments and the Global Political Economy*. London: Zed, 2016.

Menicucci, Garai. "Europe and the Political Economy of Arab Cinema." *Middle East Report*, no. 235 (Summer 2005): 46–8.

Mostafa, Dalia Said. *The Egyptian Military in Popular Culture*. London: Palgrave Macmillan, 2017.

Mouline, Nabil. "Dégage—We'Re Filming!" *Middle East Journal of Culture and Communication* 7, no. 3 (2014): 330–50.

Mulvey, Laura. *Fetishism and Curiosity*. Bloomington: Indiana University Press, 1996.

Naficy, Hamid. *An Accented Cinema: Exilic and Diasporic Filmmaking*. Princeton, NJ: Princeton University Press, 2018.

Naïm, Antonia. "'Bab el Chams' ('La Porte du soleil'), un film de Yousry Nasrallah." *La pensée de midi* 14, no. 1 (April 2005): 120–6.

Nasser, Gamal Abdul, and Walid Khalidi. "Nasser's Memoirs of the First Palestine War." *Journal of Palestine Studies* 2, no. 2 (1973): 3–32.

Peteet, Julie. *Landscape of Hope and Despair: Palestinian Refugee Camps*. Philadelphia: University of Pennsylvania Press, 2011.

Progressive Assembly of National Unionists. "No to the Egyptian-Israeli Treaty." *MERIP Reports*, no. 80 (1979): 14–18.

Roy, Sara. "De-Development Revisited: Palestinian Economy and Society Since Oslo." *Journal of Palestine Studies* 28, no. 3 (April 1, 1999): 64–82.

Radwan, Noha. "Palestine in Egyptian Colloquial Poetry." *Journal of Palestine Studies* 40, no. 4 (July 1, 2011): 61–77.

Saglier, Viviane. "'Not-Yet' an Industry: The Temporalities of Contemporary Palestinian Cinema," in *Cinema of the Arab World: Contemporary Directions in Theory and Practice*, eds. Terri Ginsberg and Chris Lippard, 125–46. Cham, Switzerland: Palgrave Macmillan, 2020.

Said, Edward. "The Burdens of Interpretation and the Question of Palestine." *Journal of Palestine Studies* 16, no. 1 (1986): 29–37.

Said, Edward. "Preface," in *Dreams of a Nation: On Palestinian Cinema*, ed. Hamid Dabashi, 1–5. London and New York: Verso, 2006.

Salem, Sara. *Anticolonial Afterlives in Egypt: The Politics of Hegemony*. Cambridge, UK: Cambridge University Press, 2020.

Salem, Walid. "The Anti-Normalization Discourse in the Context of Israeli–Palestinian Peace-Building." *Palestine-Israel Journal of Politics, Economics and Culture* 12, no. 1 (2005), https://pij.org/articles/334/the-antinormalization-discourse-in-the-context-of-israelipalestinian-peacebuilding.

Salti, Rasha. "Critical Nationals: The Paradoxes of Syrian Cinema," in *Insights into Syrian Cinema: Essays and Conversations with Contemporary Filmmakers*, ed. Rasha Salti, 21–44. New York: Rattapallax, 2006.

Samak, Qussai. "The Politics of Egyptian Cinema." *MERIP Reports*, no. 56 (April 1977): 12–15.

Samak, Qussai. "The Arab Cinema and the National Question: From the Trivial to the Sacrosanct," *Cineaste* 9, no. 3 (1979): 32–4.

Sayigh Rosemary. *Palestinians: From Peasants to Revolutionaries*, New ed. London and New York: Zed, 2007.

Sayigh, Yezid. "The Politics of Palestinian Exile." *Third World Quarterly* 9, no. 1 (1987): 28–66.

Sayigh, Yezid. "Armed Struggle and State Formation." *Journal of Palestine Studies* 26, no. 4 (1997): 17–32.

Sayigh, Yezid. *Armed Struggle and the Search for State: The Palestinian National Movement, 1949–1993*. Oxford and New York: Oxford University Press, 1997.

Schochat, Ella. "Egypt: Cinema and Revolution." *Critical Arts* 2, no. 4 (January 1983): 22–32.

Selaiha, Nehad. "The Fire and the Frying Pan: Censorship and Performance in Egypt." *TDR* 57, no. 3 (2013): 20–47.

Shafik, Viola. "Cinema in Palestine," in *Companion Encyclopedia of Middle Eastern and North African Film*, ed. Oliver Leaman, 518–32. London; New York: Routledge, 2001.

Shafik, Viola. *Arab Cinema*. Cairo: American University in Cairo Press, 2007.

Shafik, Viola. *Popular Egyptian Cinema: Gender, Class, and Nation*. Cairo: American University in Cairo Press, 2007.

Shlaim, Avi. *The Politics of Partition: King Abdullah, the Zionists and Palestine 1921–1951*. New York: Columbia University Press, 1990.

Shlaim, Avi. "Israel and the Arab Coalition in 1948," in *The War for Palestine: Rewriting the History of 1948*, eds. Eugene L. Rogan and Avi Shlaim, 2nd ed., 79–103. Cambridge, UK: Cambridge University Press, 2007.

Shlaim, Avi. *The Iron Wall: Israel and the Arab World.* New York: W. W. Norton, 2014.

Shohat, Ella. *Israeli Cinema: East/West and the Politics of Representation.* 2nd ed. London and New York: I.B. Tauris, 2010.

Soueif, Ahdaf. *In the Eye of the Sun.* New York: Knopf Doubleday, 2011.

Stein, Ewan. *Representing Israel in Modern Egypt: Ideas, Intellectuals and Foreign Policy from Nasser to Mubarak.* London: Bloomsbury Academic, 2012.

Tabishat, Mohammed. "Society in Cinema: Anticipating the Revolution in Egyptian Fiction and Movies." *Social Research* 79, no. 2 (2012): 377–96.

Taha, Amir. *Film and Counterculture in the 2011 Egyptian Uprising.* Cham, Switzerland: Palgrave Macmillan, 2021.

Takeyh, Ray. *The Origins of the Eisenhower Doctrine: The US, Britain and Nasser's Egypt, 1953–57.* London: Palgrave Macmillan, 2000.

Talhami, Ghada Hashem. *Palestine in the Egyptian Press: From Al-Ahram to Al-Ahali.* Lanham, MD: Lexington, 2007.

Ṭarābulsī, Fawwāz. *A History of Modern Lebanon.* London and Ann Arbor, MI: Pluto Press, 2007.

Tartoussieh, Karim. "Life Is Like a Bowl of Fish: *The Aquarium*, the French New Wave and the Urban Reflection of the Cairene Self." *Journal for Cultural Research* 16, no. 2–3 (July 2012): 283–96.

Thomson, Sorcha, Pelle, Valentin Olsen, and Sune Haugbolle. "Palestine Solidarity Conferences in the Global Sixties." *Journal of Palestine Studies* 51, no. 1 (January 2022): 27–49.

Weiss, Max. *In the Shadow of Sectarianism: Law, Shi`ism, and the Making of Modern Lebanon.* Cambridge, MA: Harvard University Press, 2010.

Yaqub, Nadia. "The Dupes: Three Generations Uprooted from Palestine and Betrayed," in *Film in the Middle East and North Africa*, ed. Josef Gugler, 113–24. Austin: University of Texas Press, 2011.

Yaqub, Nadia. *Palestinian Cinema in the Days of Revolution.* Austin: University of Texas Press, 2018.

Yaqub, Salim. *Imperfect Strangers: Americans, Arabs, and U.S.–Middle East Relations in the 1970s.* Ithaca, NY: Cornell University Press, 2016.

Yousef, Yousef. *Qadiyat Filastin Fi Al-Sinima al-'Arabiyyah.* Beirut: Al-Muassasah al-'Arabiyyah li-al-Dirasat wa al-Nashr, 1980.

Index

C

D

E

F

G

M

N

O

P

R

Z

CINEMA AND MEDIA CULTURES IN THE MIDDLE EAST

Terri Ginsberg and Chris Lippard

Series Editors

The purpose of this series is to demarcate and critically examine the shifting terrain of film- and media-making in the Middle East, and of practices of film and media studies regarding it, testing them both against their larger, social enabling conditions at the national, regional, and transnational levels. Titles in the series will engage recent developments in the field of Middle East film and media studies and will help point the field in an intellectually meaningful, pedagogically effective direction in relation to both current and, in some cases, significant, previously ignored older work.

The series is conceived at a moment during which Middle Eastern film and film criticism have begun to develop in new directions. Recent years have witnessed a modest increase in scholarly engagement with topics and modes of inquiry often previously considered outside academic discourse. A handful of books and special journal issues published in English over the past half-decade, focusing on specific Middle Eastern countries, such as Tunisia, Morocco, Syria, Iran, Palestine/Israel and Turkey, as well as the long-overdue establishment of cinema studies as an emerging field of academic inquiry within universities located in the Arab world indicate a preponderance of previously unproblematized issues now circulating within the field. These include critical questions from queer and transgendered perspectives about the representation of women, and from indigenous and settler-colonial studies perspectives about the representation of migrant workers and refugees, the growing importance of documentary, digital animation and hybrid shooting, the continuing influence of global cinema imperatives, and the revival of interest in militant, revolutionary and third cinema aesthetics.

To receive more information, please contact:

editorial@peterlang.com

To order books, please contact our Customer Service Department:

peterlang@presswarehouse.com (within the U.S.)
orders@peterlang.com (outside the U.S.)

Visit our website at www.peterlang.com

www.ingramcontent.com/pod-product-compliance
Ingram Content Group UK Ltd.
Pitfield, Milton Keynes, MK11 3LW, UK
UKHW021828100926
8556IPUK00003B/212

9 781433 188404